Jacob Schoenhof

The Destructive Influence of the Tariff upon Manufacture

and Commerce

Jacob Schoenhof

The Destructive Influence of the Tariff upon Manufacture and Commerce

ISBN/EAN: 9783337397517

Printed in Europe, USA, Canada, Australia, Japan

Cover: Foto ©Suzi / pixelio.de

More available books at **www.hansebooks.com**

THE

DESTRUCTIVE INFLUENCE

OF THE

TARIFF

UPON

MANUFACTURE AND COMMERCE

AND THE

FIGURES AND FACTS RELATING THERETO

BY

J. SCHOENHOF

SECOND EDITION.

NEW YORK
PUBLISHED FOR THE
NEW YORK FREE TRADE CLUB
BY G. P. PUTNAM'S SONS
27 & 29 WEST 23D STREET
1888

INTRODUCTION.

THE tariff laws of the United States all bear one and the same characteristic feature, namely, the absence of a rational foundation for their claim of "protecting" American manufacturing industries. The word "Protection" presupposes the existence of a foreign power against which protection is desired. It would be reasonable to infer that those attempting this protection should inquire into the composition of that foreign power, to wit, the industries of foreign nations, and the tariffs upon which these foreign industries are based. Had the framers of our tariff laws made such inquiry, they would have found that the starting-point of all industrial nations, from whom our industries are to find protection, is that of free raw materials. The strongest protective tariffs, like those of Germany and France, make no exception to this rule.[1] The United States, on the other hand, commence their industrial production with rates ranging from twenty to sixty per cent. on raw materials, with rates so much above the starting-point of all competing nations, that the benefits intended to accrue from protection to our industries are usually spent before they have left the raw material, and provided slight protection to crude—or half—manufactures. Nay, the raw material and half-manufacture frequently have higher rates than the article of which they form the component material. Our manufacturers in consequence of this inverted application of the protective principle are sufferers to the extent which must necessarily follow in the train of such a mistaken policy : glutted home-markets in American manufactures of lower grades and continued large importations of foreign fabrics of higher grades. The immediate aim of reform must be to right this anomaly, to place all raw materials upon the free-list (thus to gain an even starting-point with foreign competitors), and then to reduce the tariff proportionally, so as to reserve the higher protective rate for more developed and the lower rate for cruder branches.

The new tariff-law of March 3, 1883, though different from what was proposed by the Commission, varies in no material point from the old tariff, and the changes are in no wise conducive to lighten the burdens of the people or to improve the languishing condition

[1] See Appendix I.

of commerce and manufacture. The reductions are insignificant; some duties, as those on all-wool dress goods, have been raised,[1] and the taxes on raw materials remain, with immaterial changes, as heavy as they were before the revision. I have collected the data relating to the various phases of the tariff discussion, and have put them in connected form, so as to present a clear statement of this all-important issue in its bearing upon labor, commerce and manufacture.

It has been my aim to prove in these pages, from statistical facts reaching over several decades and from the conditions of competing countries, that the recognition of the following propositions as fundamental principles must underlie all attempts at tariff reform if the same be intended to benefit the whole country, give more remunerative employment to labor, and improve its conditions by making its earnings more valuable :

✓ 1. A tariff which taxes raw materials cannot be protective to manufacturing industries.

2. A tax making raw materials cost our manufacturers more than those of competing nations is practically a prohibition of the exportation of the surplus product of our manufactures.

3. Protection, fostering competition to unnatural fierceness, becomes self-destructive on account of this exclusion from foreign outlets.

4. Foreign commerce and home manufactures must decay where raw materials are taxed.

5. The carrying trade of the world must cling to that country whose trade and manufacture bear the lightest burdens.

6. Wages are not gauged by tariffs, but by the general opportunities offered by the respective countries.

7. The standard of living of the working classes determines the rate of wages.

8. Where the standard of living is highest, productive power and invention find highest development, and production is cheapest.

9. Protection is the normal condition of countries whose standard of living is a low one.

10. Free trade is the normal condition of countries whose standard of living is a high one.

---

[1] See Appendix III.

The principles contained in these propositions once recognized, the adjustment of the tariff question will be an easy matter. The want of understanding that is apparent in all discussions is attributable to an insufficient collection of material facts, and to ignorance of the correlation of certain factors that play no small part in the concert of social forces. I have endeavored to link these into the chain of evidence, which I have been collecting for a number of years, against the tariff laws of the United States.

Though it is the avowed purpose of advocates of protection to frame tariffs for the benefit of the working classes, it is easy to prove that the tariff has not only signally failed to accomplish this, but on the contrary has circumscribed employment and reduced earnings. It must be clear to all that it must be the aim of economic science to elevate the standard of life of the working classes if the science is to fulfil its mission. The removal of burdensome taxation is, therefore, the first stepping-stone to this end. It is a step of most signal importance, one that cannot be under-valued, as our present system bears heaviest on that class, which is the least capable of bearing double burdens ; taxes to support the government and taxes for protection, which does not protect. The results of nearly twenty years of high tariffs clearly show that the system has worked to the advantage of great monopolies alone. But the effort which is made to have it appear that the war tariff is upheld for the purpose stated, is in itself a tribute paid to the spirit of the times, which would not yield to the infliction of such onerous burdens, were it not in the honest belief that the workingmen's condition in life is improved thereby. To the honest adherents of this belief these pages are addressed.

Agitation alone can bring a solution. The public mind cannot accept reforms unless prepared by education and enlightenment. This can only be given by free and extended discussion, which must lead to clearing of doubts, and thus toward liberation from oppression, which has been deferred only too long. To this end discussion is invited, as silence and indifference are the deadly enemies of all reform.

> " What great gift have my brothers, but it came
> From search, and strife, and loving sacrifice."
> —EDWIN ARNOLD, *The Light of Asia*.

STATISTICAL AUTHORITIES USED.

Census Reports of the United States.
Reports of the United States Bureau of Statistics, Commerce and Navigation.
Commercial Relations of the United States, No. 23.
State of Labor in Europe, 1878.   Reports from the United States Consuls.
The Tariff laws of Germany, France, Belgium, Canada, Great Britain.
Annual Reports of the Commissioner of Labor Statistics of Mass.
   "   "   "   "   "   " of New Jersey.
Poor's Railroad Manual.
Miscellaneous Statistics of the United Kingdom, Part XI., 1883.
Financial Reform Almanac for Great Britain and Ireland, 1883.
Accounts of Trade and Navigation of the United Kingdom for 1882.
Returns of Taxes levied in the different states in Europe, ordered by House of
      Commons.
Statistical Abstract for principal foreign Countries, for Parliament.
Maurice Block, Annuaire de l'Économie Politique.
Leone Levi, Wages and Earnings of the Working Classes.
Statistisches Jahrbuch für das deutsche Reich, 1883.
Dr. Emanuel Sax, Die Hausindustrie in Thüringen.
Schnapper-Arndt, Fünf Dorfgemeinden auf dem hohen Taunus.
Das deutsche Wirthschaftsjahr 1881.   Reports of German Chambers of
      Commerce.
Gesellschaft Concordia in Mainz, Statistische Tabellen über Arbeitslöhne.

CONTENTS.

CHAPTER I.

Protectionists have, for the last twenty years, held captive a whole nation of uncommonly intelligent people. They have held them under a spell. The pied piper of Hamelin, by the sounds of his magic flute, could not have produced such wonderful effect as our high-tariff men produce by chanting their few stale tunes in the ears of a credulous people. No deep-hidden sense underlies these incantations. It is simply the art of the priest and the credulity of the hearer that make the latter accept as tenets of wisdom what otherwise would long ago have ceased to cloud the understanding of a whole people. The mystic words that exercise so great an influence are the following:

1. We are a young nation, and as such cannot compete with the older nations of Europe.

2. American labor must be protected against the starvation wages of Europe.

3. Protection is necessary to foster our home industries, and without protection our industries would decay.

I must admit that at first sight and hearing one may be inclined to accept these as proper dogmas of belief. But on closer inspection they are found to be on very ill terms with experience, figures, and facts. I will take the points in reverse order, because, though they are usually given in the above order, No. 3 is the real bulwark of protection, and the storming of the citadel implies the consequent reduction of the lesser works. If protectionists were right in their assertion, that protection is necessary to building up home industries and maintaining our position among the great commercial nations of the world, then it would necessarily follow that nations which have forsaken that policy must be on the decline, dating from the time when they adopted what our protectionists are wont to call "heretical doctrine."

Let us see what effect free-trade principles enacted into laws have had on the commerce and manufactures of England. The export of the principal articles of manufacture, starting from 1845, the year still under the influence of the patriarchal system, was as follows :

(In millions of dollars.)	1845.	1855.	1865.	1881.
Cottons and yarns	125.	168.	274.	380.
Woollens and yarns	42.	51.	122.	105.
Linens and yarns	20.	24.	55.	30.
Silks	5.	8.	7.	13.
Iron and steel	17.	45.	64.	115.
Lead, tin, copper, and brass . . .	15.	20.	30.	26.
Tools, cutlery, and implements . . .	16.	25.	45.	68.
Coal	5.	12.	20.	36.
	245.	353.	617.	775.

It was as late as 1860 that the last taxes of a protective character were abolished, consequently the full effect of entire free trade in all materials necessary for manufactures does not appear in the above tables before 1865 ; yet the exports of the above enumerated British manufactures rose within a period of ten years (ending with 1865) from $353,000,000 to $617,000,000, or seventy-five per cent. The assertions of our protectionists and of British "fair-traders" to the contrary notwithstanding, England maintains her growing trade even to our times, as shown by the list of exports of 1881. The total of exports of British manufactures has increased twenty-six per cent. within this last period, against an increase of twenty-one per cent. in the population.

Like results followed the abolition of the prohibitive tariff enjoyed by French manufacturers up to 1860, and the substitution of comparative free trade in place thereof. Next to Napoleon III and M. Rouher, who saw farther in this respect than most of their countrymen, France owes a great debt of gratitude to the indefatigable labors of Mr. Cobden. After long and most arduous working he finally succeeded in engrafting upon the Gallic trunk a sprig of Saxon common-sense. The Englishman was not basely selfish. He wished to have England's neighbors, nay, even her hereditary foe, share in the good things to whose possession she owed her commercial greatness (knowing, however, all the time, what then seemed a great secret, that in improving your neighbor's condition you better your own). But behold what followed. The exports of France, which in 1860 were \$450,000,000, attained in 1873—immediately after a devastating war—to near \$800,-000,000. Imports and exports in 1860 were \$800,000,000 ; in 1873, \$1,450,000,000. The exports of both countries consist mostly of such of the products of their home industries as we do our utmost to prevent our manufacturers from exporting, by laying a prohibitory burden upon all materials necessary to their manufacture.

British exports of manufactures are nearly \$1,000,000,000. The last census reports the total of our inflated manufacturing values as \$5,300,000,000. This sum contains \$1,670,000,000 that does not belong to manufactures,—flouring, lumbering, blacksmithing, sugar-refining (the latter embracing in materials \$144,-698,000 and in labor only \$2,875,000), coffee-roasting, slaughtering, and other similar items not usually considered manufactures, except in American census reports, intended to make a big showing before Congressional committees. We have then left about \$3,700,000,000. Reduced to English values our manufactures represent about \$3,000,000,000.

The results of both systems of taxation on the textile and metal industries, the pets of our government, are illustrated in the table given on the following page.

Here are two great divisions : the one embracing all of the textile industries that supply our clothing and all our dry goods, the other all the metal products, utensils, tools, machinery, etc., of this great nation. With very slight exceptions all of our great protected manufacturing industries are contained in this schedule. Take the swollen condition of our prices of 1880 into consideration (in proportion 2 to 1 as to English prices, so far as metals are concerned, and nearly the same as to woollens), and you will find that the English exports alone exceed by far the entire product of our great manufacturing enterprises.

On the other hand, we bought, despite our " protective " tariff, from foreign countries, mostly English, one fourth as much in metals and more than one third as much in textiles (reducing our inflated valuation to the foreign standard), as our whole over-protected manufacturing industry has produced. Our own exports melt into nothingness alongside of the huge figures of British exports in the same line of manufactures—manufactures which we foster into decay by laying a heavy burden upon the materials of which they are composed. That the proportions given are correct can be further proven by the quantities of raw materials consumed by both countries. Our "reformed" tariff has changed nothing in this matter; our industries are not relieved, and the British have all cause to rejoice that they have such excellent aiders and abettors in our "protectionists," who have again succeeded in preventing that reform that was to give us gateway to the waters of the oceans.

I will put side by side with our entire production in the special branches, the corresponding English exports and also American exports, which will give a better illustration of the effects of the respective policies than a volume of argument:

ARTICLES.	American Production, 1880.	English Exports in 1880.	American Exports in 1880.	Foreign Imports, 1880.
(1) METALS .	$672,078,000	$237,500,000	$14,116,000	$72,744,000
(a) Brass, copper, and manufact. indust., telegragh wires . . .	30,000,000	27,000,000	180,000	1,787,000
(b) Cutlery and hardware . .	38,000,000	19,000,000	1,100,000	1,900,000
(c) Firearms . .	5,700,000	6,500,000	2,286,000	830,000
(d) Foundry Products and machinery	214,378,000	50,000,000	5,700,000	1,227,000
(e) Iron and steel, tin, etc . . .	384,000,000	135,000,000	4,850,000	67,000,000
(2) TEXTILES	$521,300,000	$534,500,000	$10,216,576	$122,350,000
(a) Cotton goods.	211,000,000	375,000,000	10,000,000	30,000,000
(b) Jut: goods .	697,000	12,500,000	———	2,850,000
(c) Linen goods .	602,000	30,000,000	———	22,500,000
(d) Silk goods .	41,000,000	17,000,000	———	32,000,000
(e) Woollens, worsteds, and mixed textiles.	268,000,000	100,000,000	216,576	35,000,000

What bright prospects would open to us if the commerce of the world were thrown open to our industries, which now for want of markets are choking in their own grease! I shall show in the progress of this argument that it is only a paper wall, the paper that contains the law which taxes raw materials, that shuts us out from our legitimate position—that of rulers of the commerce of the world.

Germany presents another illustration of the correctness of these views. After long-protracted effort, Prussia finally succeeded in coaxing the three dozen assorted petty states to curb somewhat their proud spirit of independence and enter the "Zollverein." Prussia's hard work to get that "Zollverein" to accept a free tariff on raw materials lasted well-nigh up to the time when, at Sadowa, the modern Macedonians so effectively knocked the dust out of the musty wardrobe of the heirs of the "Holy Roman Empire." The effect on German manufactures and commerce was the same as in the case of England and France.

But even the "new German policy of protection" has left raw materials free. Excepting Spain, perhaps, it is only the United States who, in spite of the experience of other nations, maintain that a Chinese wall is necessary to the well-being and happiness of her people. All other nations have torn down theirs, and by so doing have almost doubled their foreign trade *per capita*. America persists in keeping up her wall. The ill effects of this seclusion our protectionists are trying to overcome by adding another story to the already towering height of the structure. Our exports of manufactures are almost nothing compared with those of other nations. We have almost nothing to offer to an outside world except the produce of the unprotected enterprise of our agriculturists. After twenty years of protection—and some very hard years were among them—our exports of articles of American manufacture were in 1880 :

Agricultural implements, clocks, etc.	$3,500,000
Cotton manufactures	10,000,000
Iron and steel manufactures, tools, etc.	12,000,000
Leather manufactures	6,000,000
Woollens and wearing apparel	700,000
All other manufactures	10,500,000
	$42,700,000

Of all our exports, about 5 per cent., or $42,700,000, were what may properly be classified as American manufactures. This amount is less than 5 per cent. of the exports of the manufacturing industries of Great Britain, whose people are not exposed to the paternal care of a protective government, but are permitted to buy their raw materials where they can get them cheapest. In 1860 we had a moderate tariff averaging 19 per cent. on dutiable goods. In 1872, a year of great commercial prosperity, we had an average tariff of 48 per cent. on dutiable goods. The two representative years compare as follows :

	1860.	1872.	Increase or Decrease per cent.
Agricultural implements, sewing-machines, etc. . . .		$5,000,000	
Copper and brass manufacture .	$1,670,000	460,000	— 18
Iron and steel manufacture, tools, etc.	5,700,000	8,500,000	+ 50
Cotton goods	10,900,000	2,300,000	— 79
Wearing apparel and woollens .	930,000	640,000	— 32
Leather and manufactures .	850,000	650,000	— 23
All other manufactures . .	3,850,000	3,050,000	— 21
	$23,900,000	$20,600,000	

The increase in imports is greatest in all articles that pay the highest rates of duty, especially in those whose raw materials are heavily protected.

Comment is unnecessary. The above figures tell us two facts with sufficient clearness. The first fact is, that protection does not exclude European manufactures from the United States. The second fact is, that protection does most effectively exclude the manufactures of the United States from the markets of Europe and the world.

In 1860 our exports of industries now protected were nearly 7 per cent. of our entire exports ; in 1872 they were not quite 4 per cent.; in 1880 they were about 5 per cent. Omitting agricultural implements and sewing-machines, which were not exported in 1860, then the decline in exports of protected goods shows $8,000,000, or 33 per cent., which is only 3 per cent. of total exports. The imports of protected articles compare in reverse ratio :

	1860.	1872.	Inc. or dec. p. cent.	Rate of duty p. cent.
Clothing	$2,200,000	$3,000,000	36	50 to 100
Cotton goods	33,000,000	35,000,000	6	35 to 75
Flax and manufactures . .	10,000,000	22,500,000	125	35 to 40
Silk and manufactures . . .	33,000,000	36,000,000	10	60
Wool and manufactures . .	36,000,000	80,000,000	122	50 to 125
Earthenware, fancy goods, leather goods, etc.	19,900,000	34,200,000	75	35
Copper, brass, tin, etc . . .	8,500,000	17,200,000	100	35 to 40
Iron and steel manufactures . .	21,000,000	55,000,000	162	50 to 200
	$163,600,000	$282,900,000	72	

CHAPTER II.

THE DECAY OF OUR FOREIGN COMMERCE IS CAUSED BY THE TARIFF.

Our merchants and manufacturers suffer most by our tariff provisions. Right before our very doors a heavy trade is done with the South American and Central American republics, the fruits of which are gathered by the subjects of the monarchies of Europe. Somebody ought to do something—invoke the Monroe Doctrine, to say the least—to make these republics acknowledge the solidarity of republican interests, and do their duty toward a sister republic—viz., buy more goods from us.

We bought of them in 1880 $176,000,000 worth of goods—coffee, sugar, woods, wool, nitrates, guano, dye-stuffs, etc.—while they took only $58,000,000 worth from us. One-third of this sum consisted of manufactures of the United States. Cotton manufactures were represented by the sum of $3,899,400. This was our share of the supply of a population equal to that of the United States ; a population that has no manufacturing industries at all, but draws this chief article of its clothing mainly from foreign countries. Of this article we grow the staple, export it to England, where it is turned into manufactures and shipped to those countries.

Brazil, of whom we buy annually $52,000,000 worth of goods, takes from us $8,500,000 ($690,000 cotton goods) in merchandise and the remainder in exchange on London, wherewith to pay for the cotton that England had to buy from us to fill the orders for cotton goods from Brazil.

Brazil purchased from England, in 1880, of cotton goods $17,000,-000, from the United States barely $700,000. Of Cuba we bought $65,000,000. We sold the ever faithful isle $11,000,000 ($4,200,-000 manufactures including $90,000 in cotton goods).

The imports of English and American cotton goods into all the Central and South American States for the year 1880, compare as follows :

.	English goods.	American goods.
Mexico	$2,406,000	$832,200
Central America	2,161,000	77,700
British Honduras	209,000	66,800
British West Indies	3,400,000	131,000
Other West Indies (including Cuba)	6,100,000	825,000
United States of Colombia	3,163,000	586,000
Venezuela	1,449,000	149,000
British Guiana	670,000	12,800
Brazil	17,180,000	687,000
Uruguay	3,081,000	52,500
Argentine Republic	4,816,000	133,600
Chili	5,162,000	217,800
Ecuador	1,020,000	104,000
Peru	418,000	24,000
	$51,235,000	$3,899,400

In other words, Great Britain sells thirteen dollars' worth of her cotton goods to these American states, colonies, and sister republics, where we place one dollar's worth of ours.

This is certainly food for serious reflection. We must get customers for the surplus products of our mills, or the next collapse will be far more disastrous in its consequences than the one which ended in 1879. There is no reason why we should not sell the bulk of the cotton goods they need to all the Spanish

Americas and Brazil. Our cotton is not protected; hence we manufacture better cottons than the English, and intrinsically as cheaply as they. And still all the States of Central and South America do not take one fourth as much cotton goods from us as Brazil alone buys from England. What can be the cause of this? It cannot be the want of shipping. Even if the Stars and Stripes do not float over all the bottoms that carry between our ports and these countries, the fact that we get $176,000,000 annually of their produce sufficiently guarantees that we can carry back as much tonnage as we bring in, and at moderate cost. We may, therefore, boldly maintain that it is not for want of ships that our exports fall so far behind, but for lack of enterprise in our manufacturers and merchants, and the cause for this in turn is to be found in the government's neglect to abolish oppressive laws and to enact progressive ones that shall lend a helping hand to our foreign commerce. This, however, is not to be wondered at. Foreign intercourse means liberality; protection means exclusion. The human mind is so constituted that it cannot be both liberal and narrow at one and the same time. The two poles of the needle can never meet.

During the bad times, between 1876 and 1879, I have seen as many as 8,000, and even 10,000 packages of cotton goods sold at one auction sale. The same process is repeating now, in 1883. Auction sales in staples of 10,000 and 15,000 cases. Of course the goods were sacrificed in order to make room in the storehouses for new goods of the same character, although the home trade had been supplied with cheap goods in advance of the season. The consequence was the same as now, depression, constantly increasing. Had they been dumped where the sea is deepest, the result would have been less disastrous to all concerned—manufacturer, jobber, retailer, and working people. In that case a few millions would have covered the loss; in piling goods upon goods, the tumble followed each new attempt with increasing disaster, and crushed all that "did not stand from under," to use a slang expression. Had we had an export trade this would have been avoided, at least in its severest phases. But why did we not send our goods to those countries? Simply because we had not learned, or not tried to learn, to accommodate ourselves to their wants. Protection has taught us to look to the country inside the big wall as our customer for our manufactures, and "if outsiders do not want the stuff as we make it, they can let it alone."

There is, however, another reason why we do so small a business; it is the absence of accommodation extended to our importers and exporters, as shown by both the letter and the spirit of our revenue laws and government regulations. Other governments, even those of the paternal type, regulated by the police officer, make such arrangements as will help foreign commerce. Germany has her free ports of entry. But even inland cities have the same advantages of a liberal system. A German importer receiving a foreign invoice leaves all his packages in the public storehouse. He takes orders on his samples, not alone in Germany, but over all Europe. As he sells his stock he takes the goods from the different packages in any quantity his trade may require, and pays duty thereon. He may go a dozen times to the Custom-house till a case is sold out, or an invoice exhausted. In this wise he can do quite a prosperous export business from the public storehouse. The German trade to the Levant and Southeastern Europe is rapidly growing, and finding all his wants—both of German and foreign production—readily supplied in any of the large trading centres of Germany, the foreign merchant looks to these for the selection of his stock. That the sale of German manufactures is benefited by the trading facilities extended to foreign goods is quite evident.

I will cite a case from my own experience, as an illustration of how advantageously this system works both to importers and exporters. Some years ago I shipped from New York some dozens of cases of my manufactures to a house in Munich. When the time for settlement approached, claims for deduction (a chief part of a German merchant's profits) came in so heavily that I refused to allow them. I resold the goods to a house in Vienna, and although there remained of each case only a portion of the original contents, even to parts of dozens, yet there was no time lost in measuring circumlocution-tape, nor was any fine or tax levied upon the transfer. This could not have been, were it not that one can take parts of cases, pay duty if for home consumption, or send them free of duty in any desired quantity to foreign countries. Without this liberal system the foreign consignor would be at the mercy of the importer unless the goods be paid for before delivery.

Consider the advantages to be derived by our merchants and manufacturers from the adoption of this system in America. There is no reason imaginable why South American buyers cannot be brought to buy European goods in American free ports as easily as Eastern merchants got accustomed to buying their French and English goods at the fairs of Leipzig and Frankfort, or at the free ports of Hamburg and Bremen. Our manufactures are frequently shipped to South America by way of London. It would hardly pay buyers from those countries to visit our markets when they can find all they need in close proximity at another end of the world.

With free raw materials we could export a variety of manufactures and make it worth their while to buy an assortment of our goods. Under existing circumstances even the extension of our railroad system into Mexico will be of use only in the sale of some of our cotton fabrics, while American woollens are being slaughtered in New York auction houses at the rate of 10,000 to 12,000 pieces in one sale. While this is going on in New York, dry-goods firms are sending travellers into Mexico, selling American cottons and English woollen goods. The cotton goods are shipped from New York, the woollens from England. With wool, shoddy, and woolwaste, iron and steel for machinery and building purposes, 50 per cent. higher, it is out of the question to consider the possibility of exporting our woollens. Consequent upon all these drawbacks it follows that shipping cannot be done by us as cheaply as by foreign nations, even if a free gift were made to us of a whole fleet of steamers. Where a cargo both ways is always sure to be obtainable, the carrying can be done at considerably lower rates than where one or the other trip has to be made in ballast.

Commerce is the twin sister of industry. Equal development of both is necessary to the healthful existence of nations. Why commerce is the Cinderella of our government may be a conundrum to some. The reason is, however, a very plain one. We all know that the " fostering of our home industries " uses up all the energies of our statesmen, so that no time is left to inquire into the real causes of the decline of our commerce.

The only remedy known to them is the nursing-bottle of "subsidy." This, however, cannot impart life to the sickly infant, dying for the want of fresh air and free motion. These *cannot* be bottled.

People indulge in the belief that our home industries are prosperous, thanks to our present high tariff. No greater fallacy has ever been produced and believed. It is a sad duty to a tender-hearted reformer to be compelled to demolish cherished notions with remorseless figures, and I beg therefore to be permitted to reserve their production for my next chapter.

CHAPTER III.

THE DEVELOPMENT OF OUR INDUSTRIES NOT DUE TO THE TARIFF. THE TARIFF REPRESSIVE RATHER THAN OTHERWISE.

We are informed, whenever the occasion offers, that our prosperity is due to protection. We must infer from this that our protectionists, who claim so many things as the results of their acts, are able in some mysterious manner to influence the sun and the soil to bring forth more bountiful crops. Were it not for our rich crops and our cheap Western lands as against a succession of bad seasons over almost the whole of Europe and the rent-ridden farmers of the United Kingdom and other countries, our prosperity would not be greater now than it was from 1875 to 1879—a period equally blessed by protection. The prostration of our industries was then well-nigh complete in almost every branch. More than one third of all blast furnaces and steel works were blown out. Failure followed failure in the iron and woollen industries—the spoiled children of a protective government. Protection could not save them from ruin. Our workingmen turned tramps for lack of employment, and vast numbers of men became pauperized. It was the "boundless West" that saved us when protection would have starved us out of house and home. Now a friend in need is a friend indeed. If our friend fails us in our need, then we do not want him at all ; we can take care of ourselves when we are well off and prosperity smiles on us.

"But protection has built up our industries." Well, let us see whether this be so. Protection, of course, has built a great many factories. The profits that protection held out caused very many men to invest huge piles of money in brick and mortar, and large dividends were made in the few good years which the investors enjoyed. Thousands became hopelessly bankrupt as soon as the tide had turned—all thanks to protection. They were simply crushed by the fruits of the mock prosperity caused by protection. Manufacturers argued : If we make a given amount of money a year with our present capacity, then we can double our profits by doubling our production. Arithmetically this reasoning was correct ; economically it proved erroneous. That siren song of protection ate up dividends, surplus earnings, and capital.

> " Methinks the waves will swallow
> Both boat and boatman anon ;
> And this, with her sweet singing,
> The Lore-Ley hath done."

But do we really owe to protection the development of our home industries ? Let us see what they were under the low tariff of 1857. The census gives the total of manufactures for

1850 as	.	.	.	.	.	. $1,019,000,000
1860 as	.	.	.	.	.	. 1,886,000,000
1870 as	.	.	.	.	.	. 4,232,000,000

While 1860 shows an increase of 85 per cent., 1870 shows 125 per cent. increase. If our protectionists state that protection caused this surplus of increase in dollars and cents of manufactures, then they have some showing. Translated into real values the exhibit will be less gratifying. Protection and money manufactured by the printing-press raised prices. The money value was greatly enhanced ; the real increase, however, had not kept up with that of 1860. Some industries were even "fostered" in a backward direction. The prices of principal commodities compared as follows :

Pig iron (cost)	.	1860.	$16 50	1870	.	.	$30 00
"	.	"	3 40	1870	.	.	4 40
4-4 Shirting, bleached (retail)			10	1868	.	.	20
Cotton flannel (retail) .		"	15	1868	.	.	31
Boots (retail)	.	"	3 40	1868	.	.	5 00
Flour (retail)	.	"	6 87	{ 1868	.	.	15 00
				{ 1872	.	.	11 50

From these figures it is evident that it is not an exaggeration to state that the cultivation of the art of growing rich by government enactment resulted in raising the prices of all commodities contained in the estimate of the census of 1870 fully 60 per cent. Deducting this inflation from the valuation of 1870, there remains of the 4,200 million dollars only 2,625 millions to be compared with the production of 1860, leaving an increase of 40 per cent. in real values against an increase of 85 per cent. in 1860. To meet the assertion of protectionists that a high protective tariff was necessary to develop our industries, I will here state that it has done nothing of the kind, and prove it by comparing the number of hands employed in the census—years 1860 and 1870 respectively—the former a year of low tariff, the latter a year in which a high tariff and cheap money had had full sway to develop our industries to an extent that must have gladdened the heart of the most insatiable protectionist. Of course, I shall select only such items as represent large interests :

	1860.		1870.	
	Hands.	Product.	Hands.	Product.
Boots and shoes . .	123,000	$92,000,000	136,000	$182,000,000
Carpets	6,700	7,900,000	12,100	21,800,000
Clothing, men's and women's	120,500	88,000,000	118,700	160,900,000
Cotton goods . . .	115,000	107,300,000	129,400	168,000,000
Cutlery and edge tools.	4,200	4,600,000	8,900	11,000,000
Hardware	10,700	10,900,000	14,200	22,200,000
Hats and caps . . .	11,700	16,900,000	16,200	24,800,000
Hosiery	9,100	7,300,000	14,800	18,400,000
Leather	26,000	75,000,000	35,000	157,000,000
Silk goods	5,400	6,600,000	6,700	12,700,000
Woollen and worsted goods	43,000	66,000,000	90,000	173,000,000
	475,300	$482,500,000	582,000	$951,800,000

The increase in the number of hands employed in all of the most important of our protected industries is equal to the increase of population, which was about 22½ per cent. in the decade. The increase in value, however, is nearly 100 per cent., or about 63 per cent. greater than the increase in hands employed. The number of hands employed by the various industries is surely better evidence, when either greater or smaller, of a rise or decline in industrial pursuits, than the valuation in dollars and cents at a time when the purchasing capacity of the dollar was reduced to so low a point as stated above. I have omitted iron from the list, as iron has always enjoyed a pretty good rate of protection, and as it will not be denied, I presume, that the great demand for iron was due to railroad-building, etc., and not to protection. In 1860 we built 1,846 miles, and in 1870 we built 6,070 miles. Out of 100,-000 of our population there found employment

		1860.	1870.
In the manufacture of Boots and Shoes.	. . . . .	388	358
" " Clothing	. . . . . .	387	310
" " Cotton goods	. . . . .	360	340

These three industries, employing two thirds of all the working men and women engaged in the production of all articles of clothing and of dry goods for the household, gave relatively considerably less employment under the fostering care of a protective tariff, than under the low tariff of 1857. Only 15 per cent. of the total mentioned above (excepting woollen goods) gave employment to 50 per cent. more hands, an increase of 23 per cent. above the increase of population. Woollen goods are the only articles that show a very large percentage of advance—whether to the advantage of the protected I shall investigate later on. One thing, however, must be clear from the figures produced, that the development of our industries, from 1850 to 1860, was as great, if not greater, under a low tariff, as from 1860 to 1870 under the high tariff. To claim fathership of an "infant" that was a full-grown youngster before the paternal claimant was even born, is a rather bold undertaking. The United Kingdom of Great Britain and Ireland gave employment at that same time (1870) to

more than three times as many working people under free trade
as we did under protection in the following industries, subject to
the Factories Acts :

Cotton goods	450,087
Woollen and worsted goods	234,687
Silk goods.	48,124
Hosiery and laces	18,062

Leone Levi's compilation contains a vastly greater number of
people employed in the above manufactures, but he includes those
employed outside of factories.

Another evidence of a relatively smaller production under our
high tariff can be adduced by a statement of the quantity of cotton consumed. In the three years of a low tariff preceding the
high tariff for protection—1859, 1860, and 1861—our mills consumed 2,700,000 bales of cotton, against 2,900,000 bales in 1869,
1870, and 1871. (This is an absolute decline, in view of the
increase of population, only partially balanced by the disappear-
ance of exports, which in 1860 exceeded those of 1870 by nearly
$9,000,000.) In the former years it did not need government
protection to induce our people to spin cotton, work the mills and
the mines, and grow rich. All they needed was the equal protection of the law, and this they were granted ; while under the
new policy monopolies of gigantic proportions grew up, and "a
tariff for the protection of American labor" has proven to be a
machine to tax the poor for the benefit of the rich.

CHAPTER IV.

THE WOOL-GROWER NOT IN NEED OF PROTECTION.

The curse of American politics, log-rolling, is also the cause of the absurdities of our "well-balanced tariff." It gave us a system of taxation that grinds every one, does cruel injury to a whole nation of working people, and good to no one except a few monopolists and tax-gatherers, and it may safely be asserted that the corruption of our politics is largely due to protection, and to the mania for government aid and subsidies engendered thereby. Self-reliance and independence are lost where large profits are more the results of legislative grants extended to industrial enterprises than of unassisted work. The lobbyist seeks, and frequently finds, an open door to executive departments, and it is doubtful whether a civil service can be thoroughly reformed that is constantly exposed to the persistent efforts of the briber. Worse, however, than this corrupting influence upon the civil service, is the effect upon legislation and the legislator. The lobbyist, the advocate of special laws, is the greatest enemy of free institutions. When a people loses confidence in its representatives, when, rightly or wrongly, the latter are held in suspicion of being the tools of private interests, then the calamity is irreparable. The briber of an officer of the government does momentary harm, while unjust laws tax generations with unjust burdens, that are the more galling the more people become conscious of the methods by which were obtained the industrial preferences and the privilege of taxing the masses for the benefit of the few. One interest is arrayed against another, as may be seen from the history of the tariff on wool and woollens. As the manufacturer wanted a higher tariff on his manufactures, the agriculturist had to be pacified. To make him willing to pay more for his blankets, flannels, and clothing, he was thrown a sop in the nature of a promised higher price for the wool he raised. But he found out to his cost that not all is gold that glitters. Wool prices were raised, but the level was raised all around. He earned more dollars, but he had to spend a great many more to obtain the same amount of goods that entered into the production of the articles for which he sold his wool. The money did not reach as far as formerly, and as a consequence he got into debt much faster than he could ever hope to get out of it.

But even his protected wool often proved a source of great risk and danger to him by that very protection which he had considered so great a boon. It is in the nature of all protection that it either stimulates over-production or invites to indolence, carelessness, and neglect. Both, of necessity, defeat the objects for which protection is imposed. Therefore, on the whole, protection must inevitably work injury to the protected.

No other reason can be adduced why wool was to be protected but compromise of conflicting interests. Wool can be grown as cheaply here as in any other country under the sun. The very variety of our climate invites to it. The Territories promise as free and cheap a yield as Australia and South America. Why make the people of all the States pay toll to the farmer of Ohio if his land becomes too valuable and expensive for pasturage and sheep-raising? With equal justice he may claim protection for his wheat because the centre of wheat-raising keeps moving to new and cheap lands. To what extent sheep-farming as an industry migrates to cheap lands, and correspondingly declines where lands become dear in consequence of denser settlements, can best be realized by a glance over the tables on the following page.

The wheat States of twenty years ago can hardly be called so now, and still they prosper and earn a fair enough yield of other and more remunerative crops. You cannot force nature with a pitchfork, nor by legislative enactment abrogate eternal laws. Ohio wool will still be wanted, as well as Territory wool, and it will command its fair price, with or without protection, as each class of wool has its own qualities necessary to manufactures. If a free tariff of wool were to kill sheep-raising, why did it not do

so when we did have an almost free tariff ? Up to 1861, grades
below 20 cents a pound were free ; above 20 cents, the duty was 24
per cent. In 1861 the tariff was changed and remained in force
till 1864 : Less than 18 cents, 5 per cent. ; from 18 to 24 cents, 3
cents a pound ; above 24 cents, 9 cents a pound. In 1866 the
present rate of duty was imposed, or rather that in force up to
the last change.

RELATION OF SHEEP-CULTURE TO FARMING IN THE PRINCIPAL
WOOL-GROWING STATES AND TERRITORIES DURING THE
CENSUS YEARS 1870 AND 1880.

States with Rapidly Increasing Populations.	Number of Sheep.		Increase or Decrease per cent.	Number of Farms.		Increase per cent.	No. Inhabitants to the Square Mile.
	1870.	1880.		1870.	1880.		
New York . .	2,181,578	1,715,180	— 21	216,253	241,053	+ 11	107.
Pennsylvania .	1,794,301	1,776,598	— 1	174,041	213,542	+ 23	96.
West Virginia .	552,327	674,769	+ 22	39,778	62,647	+ 58	25.
Kentucky . .	936,765	1,000,269	+ 7	118,442	166,453	+ 41	41.
Tennessee . .	826,783	672,117	— 19	118,141	165,650	+ 40	37.
Missouri . . .	1,352,001	1,411,289	+ 4	148,328	215,575	+ 45	30.
Georgia . . .	419,465	527,589	+ 26	69,956	138,626	+ 98	26.
Ohio	4,928,635	4,902,486	— 1	195,953	247,189	+ 26	80.
Indiana . . .	1,612,680	1,100,511	— 32	161,289	194,013	+ 20	55.
-Illinois . . .	1,568,286	1,037,073	— 34	202,803	255,741	+ 26	55.
Iowa	855,493	455,359	— 47	116,292	185,351	+ 59	30.
Michigan . .	1,985,906	2,189,389	+ 10	98,786	154,008	+ 56	29.
Wisconsin . .	1,069,282	1,336,807	+ 25	102,904	134,322	+ 31	22.

STATES THINLY SETTLED AND TERRITORIES.

Texas. . . .	714,351	2,411,887	+238	61,125	174,184	+185	6.
Kansas . . .	109,088	499,671	+358	38,202	138,561	+263	12.
Oregon . . .	318,123	1,083,162	+240	7,587	16,217	+114	1.8
California . .	2,768,187	4,152,349	+ 50	23,724	35,934	+ 51	5.6
Utah	59,672	233,121	+291	4,908	9,452	+ 93	1.75
Colorado . . .	120,928	746,433	+517	1,738	4,506	+159	1.9
New Mexico .	619,438	2,088,237	+237	4,408	5,053	+ 13	0.98

Our imports, in round numbers, were, in

	Gold Values.
1860	$5,000,000
1861	5,000,000
1862	7,000,000
1863	13,000,000
1864	16,000,000
1865	8,000,000
1866	11,000,000

In the *quasi* free years the imports were far less than in the protected ones. From 1866 to 1870 imports declined; protection had then fairly begun to bear fruit. The industry had by that time been fostered to such an extent that in 1869, according to the report of the Commissioner of Agriculture, about 8,000,000 sheep were killed (the sheep in the country being thereby reduced about 20 per cent.), because sheep-raising became unprofitable on account of the over-supply. After that wool advanced again, and the stock was increased, with the same result after a few good years. This process repeated itself about three times during the last fifteen years. The average prices of common raw wool for each of the ten years of the last decade are given by the Bureau of Statistics as follows :

1870.	1871.	1872.	1873.	1874.	1875.	1876.	1877.	1878.	1879.
36c.	35c.	26c.	23c.	22½c.	35c.	23c.	33c.	27c.	29c.

For medium Ohio fleece, washed, Mr. James Lynch reports :

1872.	1873.	1874.	1875.	1876.	1877.	1878.	1879.	1880.	1881.
65c.	63c.	51c.	53c.	50c.	43c.	45c.	35c.	55c.	49c.

In June, 1879, the price of wool was lower than any reached for a number of years. I was offered a lot of wool at twelve and a half cents, that a few months later could not be bought at double the price. The fluctuations to which the tariff for the protection of American labor subjects the prices of wool are of a nature that cannot but be disastrous to manufacturers who depend on that staple. How easy it is to manipulate an article which is cut off from the levelling influence of foreign supply is best illustrated by reference to the wool trade of 1879. A boom was created that enriched many speculators and ruined many more. In the summer and fall of 1879, when prices were lowest, the wool dealers sent their agents secretly into the wool regions to buy up wool. Manufacturers and their agents did likewise,—but all very secretly and stealthily. Neither was to know of the movements of the other. Meanwhile, the trade papers made it their special business to prophesy nothing less than a wool famine. They figured down to a pound how much wool was in the storehouses, in the factories, and on the sheep's back. They proclaimed that the farmers had no wool, so to speak. Now, of course, a farmer is but a mortal, and in spite of his innocence, knows as well as town-bred folks how to turn an honest penny. So, when buyers who had never been seen before in those regions made their appearance, one by one, like conspirators in opera-bouffe, all "good friends of the farmer," the farmer had no wool to sell. The situation was appalling ; a revival of business all around ; a great demand for woollens, and no wool. When "the good friends," over-bidding one another, had succeeded in raising the price of wool to a point where there was no reasonable hope to obtain higher points yet, the innnocents of the rural districts suddenly remembered that they had some wool ; and they did sell wool—grease, sand, and all. When the final count of the wool crop of that year of famine, 1880, was made, it compared with previous years of plenty as follows :

(These figures are from the official Report of the Bureau of Statistics.)

Fiscal year 1877	.	.	.	lbs. wool raised,	208,000,000
" " 1878	.	.	.	" "	211,000,000
" " 1879	.	.	.	" "	232,000,000
" " 1880	.	.	.	" "	280,000,000

Meanwhile, buyers were sent all over the inhabited world to buy wool. Asia, Africa, Australia, and South America were cleaned of wool to satiate the voracious maw of the American speculator. The wool merchants of London had little wool to offer, and a real scarcity made itself felt, and created a feeling of great anxiety lest the much-coveted fleece should not be obtainable at all. Our Argonauts resold a good deal of foreign wool to the panic-stricken English when the over-supply in this country began to make itself felt.

Imports of foreign wool in 1879 were . . 39,000,000 lbs.
" " 1880 " . . 128,000,000 lbs.,

in value nearly five times that of the importations of 1860.

It is an ill wind which blows nobody good. The speculators, at least, had no reason to find fault with a tariff for the protection of our home industries. The sweet nectar of the boom in woollen manufactures was not without its bitter dregs for the manufacturer, however. Large prices were asked, and large prices were obtained. Every spindle was put in motion, every card employed and driven with all the speed that modern invention could supply. Extra hands were set to work in relays. But not all the promises of the commission houses (the agents of the mills) were realized. Many dealers bought largely; others, mistrusting, held back, only supplying their immediate wants ; and a great many stocks were kept on hand that were made of high-priced wool, and had to be sacrificed at a great reduction and loss to the manufacturer.

One class of woollen goods may serve as an illustration. Felt goods, an article that brought 55 cents a yard in the early summer of 1879, was raised in the spring of 1880 to 80 and 85 cents a yard. This price promised so well that manufacturers "went in heavy." The storehouses were filled to overflowing to await the rapid sales expected by all whom it concerned. They kept on expecting, but their expectations were not to be realized. In 1881 those very goods, kept over from the boom year, were sold—the very best goods, expected to bring 85 and even 90 cents—at 50 and 55 cents. One manufacturing concern had a hundred thousand yards left over, and sold them at that reduction. Just contemplate the havoc created by protection in this one instance. The consequence was that of six felt mills in Franklin, Mass., operating in 1880, there are only one or two left now to tell the tale. The others have either failed or gone into liquidation. In other lines of woollens similar experience was made, although the consequences were of not so pronounced a character. These spasmodic changes are matters of regular occurrence.

Only a few days ago, June, 1883, an auction sale of 12,000 pieces of heavy woollens took place for want of regular buyers. But this was only the beginning in a series of forced sales of a like nature that followed shortly after in quick succession. And all this under a tariff for protection !

Napoleon said : " The world is governed three fourths by imagination."

CHAPTER V.

To many of our industries protection acts as a boomerang. Intended to crush the foreigner (the enemy of our "infant industries"), it enables foreign competition to undermine industries protected by a tariff of a hundred per cent. or more. We begin our inquiry with an article of last finish, ready for immediate use, cloaks.

Cloaks have taken for the last few years the place of shawls in woman's outfit. They are manufactured in large quantities and are represented by millions of dollars, giving employment to thousands of men and women in mills and workshops. Foreign-made cloaks, up to the late revision, have been paying a duty of 50 cents a pound and 40 per cent. *ad valorem.* In the lower class of goods this is equal to a protection of over 100 per cent. The new rate is 45 cents a pound and 40 per cent. *ad valorem.* Yet Berlin-made cloaks are annually shipped to the United States in very large quantities, excluding to that extent American-made goods, protected, as just said, at those high rates. With such protection one should suppose foreign competition practically impossible. Considering, however, the degree of protection which all materials enjoy that enter into a garment, the solution is simple enough.

1. Woollens were paying 50 cents a pound and 35 per cent. *ad valorem,* new rate 35 cents a pound and 35 per cent. *ad valorem,* and goods above 80 cents a pound 35 cents and 40 per cent. As this is the "poor man's government," it is natural enough that the poor man is taxed heaviest. On his clothing he still pays nearly double the rate of the rich man. Goods of an inferior quality and value, heavily loaded with cotton, shoddy, dye-stuffs,

etc., pay from 100 to 150 per cent.; fine goods made of pure wool
of the finest texture pay from 60 to 80 per cent.

The old and new tariffs bear the following relation :

	Old Tariff 50 cts. and 35 per cent.	New Tariff 35 cts. and 35 per cent.
A cheap cloth, costing in Germany or England, say 75 cts. a yd., weighing 28 oz. weight duty — . . . . . . and *ad valorem* duty . . .	87½c. 26¼	61c. 26¼
	$1.13¾ or 152 %	87½ or 116 %

Goods of American make, corresponding in value, sold from
first hand at prices ranging from $1.75 to $1.90 per yard. New,
desirable goods, in consequence of the recent tariff enactment, are
offered now at about $1.50.

	Old Tariff. 50 and 35 per cent.	New Tariff. 35 and 40 per cent.
2. Fine Woollens costing at the foreign place of export $2 a yard, and of like weight — weight duty . . . . . . *ad valorem* duty —	87½c. 72	61c. 80
	$1.57½ or 78¾ %	$1.41 or 70½ %

There is still a very large discrepancy between the fine and the
coarse fabrics.

	Old Tariff. 50 and 35 per cent.	New Tariff. 35 and 40 per cent.
Take finer goods, Coatings, costing 12 s. or $3. Weight 24 oz. — . . . . *ad valorem* duty — . . .	75c. 1.05	52c⅛. 1.20
	$1.80 or 60 %	$1.72½ or 58 %

The finer the goods, the lower the rate of duty ; the coarser, the higher the rate : inviting the importation of finer cloths and stimulating an over-production of coarse, unsightly, trashy goods, filling the storehouses to overflowing, only to be relieved by forced auction or sheriff's sales.

This proportion of burdens, laid upon the poor man's shoulders by a providential government, runs through the whole list of woollen goods.

3. Italian cloths, used for linings, pay the same proportion of duties.

4. Trimmings, made of wool, escape the weight duty to a certain extent, as their weight is about balanced by what falls off the material in cutting the cloth. Woollen plushes are now used most extensively for cloak trimmings, linings, and cloaks. They are imported in large quantities. The manufacturer who uses them for his American-made goods pays at the following rates :

	Old Rate. 50 and 35 per cent.	New Rate. 35 and 35 per cent.
A low quality of velour costs 18d. English—36c. Weight, 28 ounces at 50c. — weight duty *ad valorem* duty —	87½c. 12½	61c. 12½
	$1.00 or 277 %	73½ or 204 %
A fine seal plush costs 20s. English — $4.80 Weight, 28 ounces at 50c. — . . 35 % *ad valorem* —	87½c. $1.58	61c. $1.92
	$2.45 or 51 %	$2.53 or 52½ %

Silk, silk ornaments, silk laces, etc., if imported in the piece have been paying 60 per cent. and are now reduced to 50 per cent. *ad valorem*. If on cloaks, as trimmings, they only pay 40 per cent. *ad valorem*, as their weight duty is infinitesimal in proportion to their value.

5. Sewing by hand receives poorer wages than most other work in Europe ; the lesser cost of making a garment is, therefore, greatly to the advantage of the foreign manufacturer.

Under the old tariff law protection heaped heavier charges

upon the manufacturer than were remitted to him in protecting the finished goods.

> " Though this be madness, yet there 's method in it."

The new tariff gives him an even chance. To illustrate I will give an accounting of the manufacturing cost :

FOREIGN CLOAKS IMPORTED.	Old Tariff 50 cts. and 40 per cent.	New Tariff 45 cts. and 40 per cent.
a.) Cheap quality, 12 marks, $3.00 — specific 3 pounds — 40 % *ad valorem* —	$1.50 1.20	$1.35 1.20
	$2.70 or 90 %	$2.55 or 85 %
b.) Fine quality, 50 marks, $12.50, same weight 40 % *ad valorem* —	$1.50 5.00	$1.35 5.00
	$6.50 or 50 %	$6.35 or 49 %

Now let us examine into the relative cost of these two classes of cloaks, cost of component parts in Berlin, and brought to New York made-up, with duty and expenses added, and New-York-made cloaks and cost of component parts under both tariffs :

In this, my price-statement, a margin of profit is left to the cloak maker in Berlin, but none to the American manufacturer. Most of the foreign importations are consigned, and under-valuation, in the finer grades especially, frequently further discriminates in favor of foreign makers.

This may serve as an example of the kind of protection most of our highest advanced industries obtain by "our well-balanced tariff system." Were it not for the difficulty of foreign adaptation to American style and fashion, this would be one of the American industries for which an epitaph would soon be wanted. As it is, the industry is flourishing in spite of protection. The annual production of cloaks is estimated to exceed thirty millions of dollars.

	Manufacturer's Cost Price in		
	Berlin.	New York. Old Tariff.	New York. New Tariff.
a.) 2 yards Cloth	$1.50	$3.70	$3.00
¼ yard Satin or Silk	25	40	37½
Buttons and Italian Cloth	15	30	30
Making	35	65	65
Factory Expenses	15	50	42½
Discount	15	30	30
Profit	45	. . . . .	. . . . .
	$3.00	$5.85	$5.05

	$3.00	$3.00
Berlin Cloaks landed in New York, old tariff rate	2.70	new rate 2.55
Total	$5.70	$5.55

	Berlin.	New York. Old Tariff.	New York. New Tariff.
b.) 2 yards Cloth	$4.00	$7.15	$6.82
Silks and Fringes	4.00	6.40	6.00
Buttons, etc.	1.00	1.00	1.00
Making	1.00	2.00	2.00
Factory Expenses	75	1.75	1.50
Discount	75	1.25	1.25
Profit	1.00	. . . . .	. . . . .
	$12.50	$19.55	$18.57

	$12.50	$12.50
Berlin Cloaks landed in New York, old tariff rate.	6.50	new tariff 6.35
Total	$19.00	$18.85

CHAPTER VI.

THE TARIFF ON WOOL AND RAW MATERIALS THE ONLY CAUSE OF OUR INABILITY TO COMPETE.

But why not reduce the tariff on woollens to relieve the cloak manufacturers? Well this is an equally simple story. The manufacturer of woollens is not much better off than the cloak maker. See what a load he has to carry.

(1) Raw wool has been paying 10 cents a pound and 11 per cent. *ad valorem.* The shrinkage extends often to 65 per cent. On scoured wool the tariff-charges were 30 cents a pound and 33 per cent. *ad valorem,* or three times the rate of grease wool. A pound of foreign-grown wool has cost accordingly from 35 to 40 cents more before being used by an American spindle than it cost an English spindle to spin it into yarn.

Under a general weakening of wool prices, American wools had come down to within two to three cents of the full foreign price inclusive of duties and charges. This has induced the Tariff Commission to recommend and Congress to enact the abolition of the *ad-valorem* tax on wool. The specific tax remains unchanged : ten cents on a pound of wool grease and dirt. (To offset this great sacrifice, the price limit has been reduced and all wools over 30 cents have to pay 12 cents a pound as against the same rate on wools over 32 cents, as before. These finer grades are the wools we are mostly in need of to diversify our fabrics, but are excluded under this almost prohibitory measure. But the infants are very much chagrined, even with this concession, at that ruinous reduction, as they say, and threaten the formation of a national organization to agitate a restoration of the old rates.) This reform measure leaves the American wool manufacturer in his wool supply in the following position toward his foreign competitor : (Table furnished by Mr. James Lynch.)

Description.	Shrinkage, per cent.	Rendered, per cent.	Lb. grease, duty, cents.	Price at place of export.	Percentage duty on pound grease wool.	Value scoured, England.	Amount of duty on lb. scoured wool.	Percentage of duty on each pound scoured wool.
Buenos Ayres . . .	70	30	10	13c.	77	43½	33½	77
Montevideo . . .	56	44	10	20c.	50	43¾	22¼	56¼
Cape of Good Hope.	66	34	10	16c.	62½	46.2	29.2	63½
Port Philip . . .	56	44	10	27c.	37.2	61¼	22¾	37⅞

After this great and liberal reduction of 11 per cent. the tariff remains yet 37½ to 77 per cent. *ad valorem*—fully equal to if not higher than the original war tax. Just think of it—37½ to 77 per cent. tax on a raw material, wool, that is imported free of duty by all industrial nations, not by any means as favorably situated as we are for the production of this most necessary staple. Of course, the lowest grades pay the highest duties, as in all enumerations of our wonderful tariff.

Foreign wools have declined in price since the war tariff was imposed, so that even with this reduction the percentage is on the average fully as high as it was ten years ago, as will be seen by this table :

Hellmuth Schwarze's London Price List.	Description.	1872.			1882.		
		Pound grease duty.	Price at place of export.	Per cent. of duty.	Pound grease duty proposed.	Price at place of Export.	Per cent. of duty.
	Buenos Ayres	10 cts., and 11%	16	73½	10	14	71⅛
	Peru, middling	"	30	44⅛	10	22	45⅜
	Eastern, Cape of Good Hope	"	32	42¼	10	24	41⅞
	Port Philip, average fleece .	12 cts., and 10%	34	45	10	24	41⅜

After England, we are now the largest wool-consuming nation. Our exclusion of foreign wools naturally throws all the advantages of depressed foreign markets into the hands of the foreign, principally English, wool-spinner. We act as this depressing influence, which the foreign manufacturer is using with telling blows against our own industries, despite all our efforts at protection. Given free wool, the price on the other side would advance and prevent our foreign competitors from ruling the markets of the world, both as buyers of wools and sellers of wollens.

(2) Shoddy, woollen rags, mungo, and wool waste pay 10 cents (formerly 12 cents) a pound, fully 50 per cent. of the foreign price.

(3) Dyestuffs, chemicals, and other ingredients cost our manu-

facturers fully 50 per cent. more on the average than their English competitors have to pay.

(4) Coal (bituminous) pays a duty of 75 cents a ton. This precludes the New England manufacturer from using the coal of the adjacent coal-fields of the British possessions, and enables the Pennsylvania owner of coal mines and transportation lines to charge "what the market will fetch."

(5) Heavy machinery composed of iron that pays $6.72 a ton, or 60 per cent., bar-iron 75 per cent., and steel that pays 45 per cent., costs vastly more than English machinery.

The cost of factory buildings and machinery is fully double that of the English mills; interest charges, etc., consequently, more than twice as high as those of the British manufacturer.

With not one half the means of circulation at her command, the industrial production of England, per capita, is nearly twice that of ours.

Our inflated prices, largely due to the tax on raw materials, cause a constant sharp demand for money, and a consequent higher rate of interest. All of which burdens add heavily to our cost of production, without furthering the condition of manufacturers and laborers one iota.

It would be a moderate estimate to say, that protection adds fully 75 cents to the cost of a yard of 6-4 cloaking that is now sold in this market at prices ranging from $1.75 to $2.

Our woollen manufacturers could at once compete with the foreign manufacturer under a moderate tariff, of not more than 25 per cent., if they had not this tremendous dead weight (of taxes on raw material, dyestuffs, machinery, etc.) to carry. But they cling frantically to a delusion. They imagine that they would be drowned without protection, and do not see that the threatening waves are an hallucination of their excited brains.

Our imports in woollens in 1880 amounted to $35,000,000, about the same as in 1870.

Our production in the latter year was $173,000,000. Duty, charges, and gold premiums, added to the imports, gave them (at the lowest average, 65 per cent. duty, 5 per cent. charges, 15 per cent. premium) a currency value of nearly $70,000,000. In other words, we imported $40 worth for every $100 worth which we manufactured, at a time when we were most thoroughly protected by a tariff imposed to exclude foreign woollens.

In 1882 we imported $38,000,000, adding duties and charges, then this is fully equal to 30 per cent. of the extraordinary production of the boom year with its largely inflated prices in woollens and worsteds; inclusive of all the low, mixed textiles of which our mills are such prolific producers.

In fine goods we cannot compete with foreign nations in our own markets, as may be gathered from the computation of specific rates, given above. The consequence is, that our manufacturers turn their attention almost wholly to one and the same class of goods—with what results can be learned from the long list of failures in our woollen industries during the last ten years.

Even now, after two years of prosperous trade, following the long depression, we are again verging on a repetition of that disastrous period, when woollen mills were sold under the hammer and went begging for buyers at one quarter their original value.[1]

This is what protection is doing for our woollen industry. Well may protectionist apostles proclaim that "protection" reduces prices. The sentence can have but one meaning, namely, that protection invites an excess of capital and labor into protected enterprises, and ultimately ripens thereby so keen a competition that ruin follows to all concerned in these industries. At best, a proceeding of a decidedly questionable morality, if this is the conscious aim of our protectionists. The consumer, however, is reaping small benefit from this "price-reducing character of protection." The tax on raw material is sufficiently high, and its prices are so easily kept to their full limit, that ruin may overtake the producers of articles made of these raw materials, and yet no perceptible relief be given to the consumer. But even the farmer is not benefited, though he is made to believe that his interest is pre-eminently advanced by this wool tax. The farmer and the sheep-raiser by no means represent the same interest. A

---

[1] According to a careful estimate, about 60,000 cases of American dry goods, cotton and woollen goods, have been sold at public auction and at ruinous prices since the opening of the fall season till September, 1883; each succeeding sale bringing poorer returns than the former. But they continue to be brought on as the only means of relief of an over-production that has no other outlet than an overburdened home market.

correct review of the case must convince the farmer that he is the loser in the game. We raised in the census year 35,000,000 sheep, more or less, distributed among 4,000,000 of farmers, which number, evenly divided, would give each farmer nine sheep. Now it is a known fact that all States whose lands become valuable on account of denser settlement, decrease the number of their sheep ; as sheep-culture, on a scale larger than that required for the raising of mutton, becomes unprofitable with the development of agri-culture. Wool then is considered an incidental profit only.

The large wool-growers use the millions of farmers who produce little wool simply as cat's-paws to get their chestnuts out of the fire. The burdens which every farmer has to carry as a consumer of woollen goods, are at least four times as high as the amount he would get more for his wool, if all sheep raised in the United States were equally divided among each and every farmer. They would get nine sheep each. These nine sheep give about fifty-five pounds of raw wool, which, at a protection of ten cents, gives him $5.50 protection. His clothing and woollen wear for himself and family cost him an average of fully $50, which $50 is about twice what he would need under free wool. Consequently, in woollen goods alone he has to pay a tax of $25 from his earnings, while his imaginary earnings from sheep-raising average only $5.50. I do not add to this calculation the high price of his tools, of his machinery, his agricultural implements, and household utensils, which are equally enhanced in price by this obnoxious system of tariff legislation.

The wool clip of the United States, taking the highest estimate, is about 250,000,000 pounds, raw. Averaging the whole, high and low grades, at 30 cents a pound, will give us an aggregate of $75,-000,000. Our woollen industry—manufacturers' value—is $267,-000,000. Ready-made clothing, woollen shirts, cloaks, etc., manufactured out of these goods, amount now to fully $250,-000,000. We have, therefore, industries amounting in the aggre-gate to over $500,000,000, whose very existence is based on this raw material and its liberal supply at reasonable and stable prices. The woollen industries employ 167,000 persons ; the ready-máde clothing and other kindred industries fully 250,000. Manufactur-ing interests of over $500,000,000 and the daily bread of nearly half a million [1] of working people depend upon this staple. A tax of ten cents a pound on raw wool amounts for this large clip to only $25,000,000. To pay a bounty of ten cents a pound to the sheep-raiser, admit wool and its substitutes free, and take this disturbing element—tax on wool—out of our manufacturing industries and commercial relations, would be less of a national waste than the present system. A tax on raw materials is not like a tax on finished goods. A tax on raw materials is equal to its own amount, plus the usual percentage of gross profit, multiplied by the number of procedures through which it has to pass until it reaches the consumer in the finished state. A protection of $25,000,000 on wool keeps swelling and swelling at each intermediate stage until it reaches the consumer, and may be called nearer a hundred million of dollars when it goes into consumption in its most finished state, without any adequate advantage to manufacturer, workingman, or consumer. I do not see why all these interests should be sacrificed to the maker of the raw material. His plant is the free soil of the prairie and the genial sky of the United States. The manufacturer is differently situated. He has large interests at stake. He cannot stop his works at will. Very frequently the existence of a whole village depends on one mill. A stoppage of work is like the failing of crops in agricultural districts. If protracted, the organization will have to disband, the workmen will have to find other employments outside of their wonted circle, or they and their dependents would perish from starvation. The manufacturer, on the other hand, if he permitted their migration, would find himself without hands if reviving demand should call for the renewed activity of his factory. Hence he often keeps his mill going at a great loss. All these considerations are foreign to the wool-grower. His help is easily replaced. His machinery is not eaten by rust. He can easily keep his product within the limits of demand without injurious effects to any one. Why then consider protection for him any more necessary than for the beef-raiser, the pork-raiser, the grower of corn, wheat, and cotton, and for all the cultivators of our free soil ?

---

[1] Counting three dependents to one wage earner, they represent a population of two millions.

Therefore, if any aid were needed, I should invoke it for the *manufacturer and his help*, but not for the raw material.

Protection of industries and taxes on raw materials cannot co-exist. Taxes on raw material inevitably lead to decay of manu-facturing industries. Either one or the other has to give way. There is no choice, no alternative. If our industries are to lead an active, healthy life, then all and every tax from raw materials has to be taken off the statute-book. No scaling-down-horizontal-reduction will do. The beginning must be made at the bottom of the structure. When once introduced this reform will work wonders. Our manufacturers will then show in a very brief time how easily they can compete with Europe. They will learn that the lowest rates are more protective than the present " protective system."

CHAPTER VII.

THE TARIFF ON STEEL RAILS A FURTHER ILLUSTRATION OF THE EFFECTS OF PROTECTION. ALSO A BRIEF HISTORY OF THE GREAT SLAUGHTER OF THE INNOCENTS BY THE COMBINED BRITISH CAPITALIST.

Protectionists, in arguing their case, remind one of the hare of Baron Munchausen, who eluded all the attempts of that famous hunter to hunt him down. Finally, the Baron discovered that the hare had two sets of legs—one set below, like all honest quadrupeds, and another set on his back. When he got tired on his ordinary legs he turned over and continued the run on his spare legs.

One argument of the protectionists is, that protection is needed for the protection of our working classes and manufacturers. When pressed with the rejoinder that the rise in the prices of all commodities counterbalances the advantages of higher wages, then they put themselves on their spare legs and point with pride to the influence of the tariff to reduce prices. Absurd as this argument may appear, it is, nevertheless, used altogether too frequently not to call for refutation. If the tariff acts in this way, then why have a tariff? If protectionists admit that its principal function is not performed—viz., the function of maintaining prices and their necessary consequence—high wages,—then the sooner we abolish it the better for all concerned.

The protectionists simply give up their case as hopeless when they bring this evidence into court. Prices, of course, have been cheapened, as shown before. They are in all industries cheaper than during the springtide of protection. Prices always work toward a common level—cost of production plus a moderate profit. They do it the more quickly the more influences are at work to stimulate over-production ; and a protective tariff is such an influence. Prices, however, can never reach a true level, that of foreign competition, while raw materials are protected. Our prices may become low enough to ruin all manufacturers, and still be higher than those at which foreign manufacturers can work at a profit and export their surplus.[1]

The injurious influence of a high tariff is further visible in the fluctuations of prices. At times of great demand prices are apt to be raised to the highest rates which the tariff allows, to be reduced again at times of stagnation to a correspondingly low figure. When patent rights exclude home competition, prices, of course, can be more easily maintained up to the importing price. Steel rails and all steel made on the Bessemer process are manufactured by a great monopoly.

The right to manufacture Bessemer steel in the United States is owned and exercised by "The Bessemer Steel Company, Limited," which is a consolidation of former organizations and owners of various patents, both foreign and American, including the Bessemer and Kelley patents. Although the Bessemer patent has run out, still all later improvements and inventions governing this process, and protected by patents, have been bought and are now owned by this same company. Under the above monopoly thirteen works were running and two additional ones were erected in 1881. The monopolists owning these patents were, by virtue of this ownership, enabled to get all that the tariff allowed them to take—that is, the price of the foreign article plus duty and charges for railroad and ocean freight, commission charges, and inland transportation, which I compute as, on the average, $7 a ton. The duty, a specific duty, up to July 1st, 1883,—$28 a ton ; consequently, after fifteen years of its existence, was thrice as high as at the time when the tariff charge was enacted, the prices of foreign rails having come down to about a third of their original cost. Our prices simply had to follow English prices in their decline. Our steel men did not do any thing more than yield to the inevitable.

Let us compare prices and find out what the tariff has done in this instance : 1868—American rails, currency, $158. English rails, gold, $61.50 ; duty $28 ; charges and freight, $7 ; gold premium, 40 per cent.; currency price, $135.

---

[1] *All* industrial nations, whether of a free-trade or protective character, admit raw materials free of duty. This sorry distinction is left wholly to the people of the United States. See Appendix I.

Here we have a larger discrepancy than in later years. Steel rails in that year were not produced in large quantities—2,500 tons. The price of $158 is, therefore, largely illusory, especially as the price of an article that fluctuates so largely as steel rails cannot be given with any degree of accuracy, and where one price, the English, may have been noted at one period and the American at another period of the year. But they come close enough to show the relative bearing to one another.

	American Steel Rails.	English Steel Rails.				
	Currency.	Gold.	Duty.	Freight.	Gold Premium per cent.	Currency Price.
1869 . . .	$132 00	$55 00	$28	$7	.33	$120
1870 . . .	106 75	51 00	28	7	.15	99
1871 . . .	102 50	55 00	28	7	.12	102
1872 . . .	112 00	67 00	28	7	.10	112
1873 . . .	120 00	80 00	28	7	.8	123
1874 . . .	94 00	68 75	28	7	. .	110
1875 . . .	68 75	44 28	28	7	. .	85
1876 . . .	59 25	32 00	28	7	. .	70
1877 . . .	45 50	29 00	28	7	. .	66
1878 . . .	42 25	23 00	28	7	. .	60
1879 . . .	48 25.	25 00	28	7	. .	60
1880 . . .	67 50	35 00	28	7	. .	70

Now compare supply and demand of corresponding years :

	Home Production.		Imported Rails.		Miles of Railroads Built.
	Iron. Tons.	Steel Rails. Tons.	Iron. Tons.	Steel. Tons.	
1868 . . .	459,500	2,500	163,000		2,979
1869 . . .	584,000	7,200	313,000		4,615
1870 . . .	586,000	34,000	399,000		6,070
1871 . . .	737,500	38,200	566,000		7,379
1872 . . .	906,000	94,000	381,000	150,000	5,878
1873 . . .	761,000	129,000	99,000	160,000	4,107
1874 . . .	584,000	145,000	8,000	100,000	2,105
1875 . . .	502,000	291,000	1,000	18,000	1,712
1876 . . .	467,000	412,000	287	. . . .	2,712
1877 . . .	333,000	432,000	. . . .	. . . ,	2,281
1878 . . .	323,000	550,000	. . . .	. . . .	2,687
1879 . . .	420,000	683,000	19,000	25,000	4,721
1880 . . .	494,000	954,000	132,000	158,000	7,174

From 1869 to 1873 railroad building had assumed proportions far in excess of any thing previously experienced. Neither our iron nor steel works, then in their infancy, were able to satisfy the enormous demand. From 1869 to 1873 we built 28,000 miles of our roads, against 9,000 miles for the preceding five years and 6,000 miles for the five years from 1859 to 1863. In the five years following 1873—the panic year—railroad building was reduced to a little over 11,000 miles. The demand from 1869 to 1873 drew increasingly from foreign supply. We imported 2,000,000 tons of iron and steel rails and manufactured 3,850,000 tons. During this period, when we had a supply of near 6,000,000 tons, the price of the home product was kept up to the price of the foreign article, plus import duty and charges. For the five years after the panic our importations only amounted to 118,000 tons of steel rails and 9,000 tons of iron rails ; total, 127,000 tons. And this importation took place during the first two years of the period. During the succeeding three years importations entirely ceased.

The demand was 60 per cent. less than through the previous period. This and increasing means of supply by the home plant caused a corresponding reduction in prices, irrespective of foreign prices. In view of such facts it is rather startling to meet frequently with statements of which the following may serve as an example :

" Prior to the manufacture of Bessemer steel in this country, the lowest price at which steel rails could be imported was $150 per ton. At that price American manufacturers knew that they could profitably compete with the world, and, accordingly, enterprising proprietors of American iron-works invested very large sums of money in the purchase of patents under which alone such rails could be produced. But when they came to put the rails upon the market they were met with the best quality of British rails at $120 per ton. Their capital was invested, and so their first sales were at the latter price. Their foreign rivals, with an enormous combination of capital, knew the value of the American market, and determined to retain it, and offered the rails at $100—American manufacturers, with all their science and mechanical skill, could not overcome this competition of the combined iron-masters of Great Britain, and hence it was deemed absolutely necessary to

invoke the protection of the government to the labor and enterprise of its citizens, who were yet in the infancy of this new production."

The very reverse took place. The gold price of steel rails in
England ran from $55 in 1869 and $51 in 1870 to $80 in 1873,
and our prices were raised to the same level, adding duty and
charges. When the demand had slackened, our steel-masters
reduced their prices to half-way between the foreign price at the
works, and that with the duty and charges added, wisely considering that half a loaf is better than no bread at all. Consequently, it was not that the "combined capital of England"
stepped forth to assault our "struggling infant industry," but that
that very ogre John Bull took good care to get all he could for
his wares, and by no action of his were our great beneficiaries
prevented from raising theirs accordingly, from, say $100 gold in
1869 and $92 gold in 1870 to $102 gold in 1872 and $112 gold in
1873. After the collapse of 1873 that same wicked Britisher and
combined capitalist did not reduce the price of his rails to a
point sufficiently low to allow them to be imported and to compete with ours, but he kept up his price, and even then, after our
demand had ceased, he took all he could get from his other customers, and a very sharp decline took place only then when these
other customers had also been forced by collapses and crashes to
forego railroad building for a while.

When in 1879 railroad building had taken a new great start,
then the same John Bull raised the price of his merchandise from
$25 to $35, and our poor struggling steel men followed in his
wake, and the price of their goods was raised from $48 to $67 and
$70, and for a brief period even to $90—the full pound of flesh the
tariff allowed them to take.[1] These are the facts lying behind that
great conspiracy of the "combined iron-masters of Great Britain"
that plays so important a part in the argument for protection of
our "infant industries." Alas for human ingratitude! Twice in
the course of a decade our arch-enemy had an opportunity to kill
and destroy our "infant"; or at least to stunt its growth, by keeping British prices down to the low figures that were ruling in England, before the American booms had set in. But with singular

[1] The close adaptation of American prices to English prices at times of great

generosity and self-restraint, characteristic of his noble qualities of mind, the Briton forbore to make use of this golden opportunity to rid himself of a rival, and gave instead, free vent to his virtuous impulse of making all the money he could out of the revival of trade. "Truly," as Ernest Renan says of the Jews, "this is the way things always go : if one works for humanity, one may be sure to be robbed first and then to be kicked in the bargain."[1]

This is about the only industry to which protection proved of enormous benefit. Their monopoly enabled the Bessemer-steel-makers to regulate the supply so as to make the tariff pay them all it promised, and it must be said that they made good use of their opportunity. The Vulcan Steel Works at St. Louis are reported to have received $400,000 during the hard times from the combination as a bonus for not running their works. It is not mentioned that the workingmen received any wages during that time of enforced idleness. When we shall be informed on good authority that they were paid their share out of that common fund, then I will score one in favor of protection.

While rails in 1880 had within a year risen from $42 to $90, the present price, September, 1883, is $38.[2] This decline is not at all demand, can best be followed up by reviewing the monthly quotations of both during the boom :

		American Steel Rails.	English Rails in New York.		
				Duty, etc.	Full Price.
	1879.				
October 2		$50 00	$23 to 25	35	$60
October 23		50 00	24 to 27	35	62
November 13		60 00	24 to 27	35	62
December 1		63 00 — 66 00	32 to 37	35	70
	1880.				
January 1		70 00 — 72 50	—	—	—
February 5		85 00 — 90 00	50 to 55	35	85 — 90
March 4		79 00 — 81 00	46 to 50	35	80 — 85
April 1		76 00 — 80 00	46 to 50	35	80 — 85
May 6		65 00 — 70 00	38	35	73
June 10		58 00 — 60 00	30	35	65
July 1		58 00 — 60 00	28	35	63

(From the *Iron Age*).

[1] " C' est toujours ainsi que les choses se passent : quand on travaille pour l' humanité, on est sûr d' être volé et, par dessus le marché, d' être battu."

[2] Some Sales are reported as low as $35.00.

due to any concerted action of our hereditary foes on the other side of the Atlantic Ocean. English rails are now about £5, or round $25. Under the old tariff, they would have cost nearly $60, to be laid down at American competing points, and would cost from $48 to $50 under the revised tariff. The increased output of vastly augmented plant, lured into existence by colossal profits, has brought prices to this tumble, and some mills that had spread too much were exposed to failure and ruin. Thousands of working-men are consigned to their homes to cogitate over the insufficiency of tariffs to provide bread for their families, when mills have to shut down for want of markets for their goods.

CHAPTER VIII.

THE AUTOCRATS OF THE TREASURY MAKE DECISIONS THAT
ARE PLEASING TO THE INFANTS. THE LATTER PACK COM-
MISSIONS WITH THEIR OWN MEN, AND CONGRESSIONAL COM-
MITTEES ACT AS THEIR PLIANT TOOLS. BUT THERE IS
MANY A SLIP BETWEEN THE CUP AND THE LIP. ALSO AN
ACCOUNT OF A DIVISION OF PROFITS BETWEEN THE INFANTS
AND THEIR WORKMEN.

In the preceding chapter I have shown what the tariff compels the country to pay for steel rails, in excess of natural prices, to a gigantic monopoly, under favorable circumstances. Bad as the indictment stands for the tariff, worse remains to be told. The famous Bloom question is an illustration of what the country has to expect yet from this instance in class-legislation.

When the tariff was framed, the Bessemer process was hardly known in this country. It was just about being introduced in very feeble attempts. The English works were far behind what the industry became later on. The cheapening influence of the new process had not made very great strides, and prices were still very high. Taking $80 as a fair average price for English Bessemer rails, then $28 is just 35 per cent. *ad valorem*. Farther on, the tariff acts from 1865 to 1870 all enumerate as follows (based on the value of crucible steel) : Steel in ingots, bars, coils, and sheets, if valued at 7 cents or less per pound, duty 2¼ cents per pound, which is about 35 per cent.; if above 7 cents, and not more than 11 cents per pound, duty 3 cents per pound, averaging again 35 per cent.; valued above 11 cents per pound, duty 3½ cents and 10 per cent., equal to about the same rate in the meaning of the law ; in any other form not otherwise provided, 30 per cent.; and manufactures of steel, not otherwise provided for, 45 per cent.

I have been trying to be very exact in this statement, because

I wish to impress on the reader's mind that, although the duty on steel is a specific one, yet it is apparent from the figures given in the act that it was never meant to be more than from 30 to 35 per cent. *ad valorem* on steel in its cruder forms and 45 per cent. on manufactures of steel. As a rule tariff laws are not enacted on hypothetical cases that may arise, but are based on facts and figures as they do exist and as they are known to the commercial world. The tariff was not meant in this instance to be any thing more than 30 per cent., or at the utmost 35 per cent. Manufactures of iron, including machinery, are rated at 35 per cent., and manufactures of steel, including machinery and tools wherein steel is used, are rated at 45 per cent., *ad valorem*. Wherever an *ad-valorem duty* is mentioned in the various acts, machinery and tools, with all the skill and labor required for their production, are taxed 45 per cent. against crude steel at 30 per cent.

Judge French, Assistant Secretary of the Treasury, in a Treasury decision on appeal says :

" The intent of the law of 1864, regulating the duties on iron and steel, seems to have been to impose a duty of thirty to fifty per cent. upon the coarser articles of steel, although the reduction in value of steel, consequent, in part, upon improved processes of manufacture, has greatly changed the symmetry of the original act. The decisions of the department from 1867 to the present time have regarded steel blooms as subject to the duties imposed upon manufactures of steel, and upon the faith of these decisions parties have entered into large business transactions ; and the department is still of opinion that this classification is correct, and therefore adheres to such decision."

All this must be conclusive evidence that no higher rate of duties on steel in its cruder stages of manufacture was contemplated by the framers of the law than 30 per cent.

Had the duty been an *ad-valorem* duty—equal to the rate as levied when the Bessemer steel process was really in its infancy, *i. e.*, 30 per cent.—then the tariff would have been on

Railroad bars	.	.	.	$7 00	instead of	. . .	$28 00
Ingots	.	.	.	6 00	instead of	. . .	50 00
Billets	.	.	.	7 50	instead of	. . .	50 00
Bars	.	.	.	9 00	instead of	. . .	50 00

Now, not all stages of steel manufacture are mentioned in the tariff. Steel blooms are not so enumerated. They are the first stage of progress from the ingot. They enter into all sorts of manufactures from a rail to a machine. According to the tariff act they could not come under any different classing than at the rate of 30 per cent. or 45 per cent. The latter rate was the one assessed for a number of years. An importing firm opened the way for the importation of steel blooms by making inquiry at the department before they engaged in the importation. They were informed that that was the rate of duty under the ruling of the Treasury Department. The first and subsequent importations were passed and continued to be passed at that rate (45 per cent.) for several years, from 1879 to 1881. With the upstart of business in 1879 so large a demand in rails sprang up that the Bessemer mills could not produce the steel so fast as they could roll it into rails, and they were using foreign steel in addition to their own product, and they took the blooms at that rate of duty. Soon, however, they desired a new deal. They were willing enough to have blooms that had the required dimensions for rails entered as blooms, at 45 per cent., but wanted all smaller sizes, from five inches down, appraised as bars, or at a rate of 200 per cent. The same Assistant Secretary of the Treasury, Judge French, in a very accommodating spirit consented to the modest request, and gave a decision in distinct contradiction of his former ruling, in which he had said :

" Blooms may be of various qualities and shapes, according to the purposes for which they are intended. If intended for the manufacture of small articles, as tools and cutlery, the bloom may be small, and is then reheated and further rolled and hammered and cut into pieces of convenient size for handling, known as billets."

So "blooms may be of various qualities and shapes according to the purposes for which they are intended," and be blooms still and pay 45 per cent. Yet on the 5th of October, 1881, in a letter of instruction to the Collector of the Port of Philadelphia, Assistant Secretary French confirms the decision of the Collector, classifying 3½ in. blooms as steel in bars dutiable at 2¼ cents a pound. This new decision was not very advantageous to the Treasury of the United States. Judge French must have been aware of the consequence of such a decision, as he says in his decision of 1879 : " But this duty " (mentioning then a much smaller one—1¼ cents) " would be prohibitory, and should not be adopted, unless the demands of the law imperatively require it." The law did not require any such distinction. The majesty of the law was not offended by calling blooms what they were christened—blooms. Why these sudden pangs of conscience?

The importers, not satisfied with this discrimination, appealed to Judge Folger. He relieved blooms down to five inches only, stating that he could not, under the law, reverse former decisions of the Treasury Department, but admitted that all blooms ought to be passed at 30 per centum, at which rate he would have all blooms classified if he were not prevented from doing so by the erroneous decisions of his predecessors.

Now, gentle reader, you will begin to see the purport and meaning of those innocent-looking measures, known as the McKinley bill of 1882, and the Tariff Commission bill of that year (which was simply a second and more comprehensive attempt of the rings to rush their measures through Congress), with their proviso that all unclassified raw materials and crude manufactures shall pay the highest rates levied on the specified articles.

The McKinley bill read as follows :

" Be it, etc., enacted that Title 33 of the Revised Statutes be amended by adding to Schedule E of said title, the following :

" Provided that on all iron and steel and on all manufactures, wares, vessels, and articles of iron or steel, or of which such metals or either of them shall be the component part or material of chief value, whether wholly or partially manufactured, there shall be levied, collected, and paid no less rate of duty than the duty or rate of duty imposed upon said goods, or upon any part or material of said goods, in any of the forms in which it or they last existed prior to their passing into the form or article on which the duty is to be levied.

" This act shall not apply to nor in any manner affect the articles specifically enumerated in this title by their commercial designation, but shall only apply to the articles designated in this title as manufactures of steel or of which steel shall be a component part not otherwise provided for ; steel in any form not otherwise provided for ; manufactures, articles, vessels, and wares not otherwise provided for of iron, or of which iron shall be the component material of chief value ; metals unmanufactured not otherwise provided for ; and castings of iron not otherwise provided for."

In plain English, the meaning of the bill was this : " That all articles designated in this title as manufactures of steel, or of which steel shall be a component part, not otherwise provided for, —steel in any form not otherwise provided for "—shall hereafter pay a tax of 100 to 200 per cent. to the Bessemer-steel-makers, instead of the 30 per cent. that was originally laid on steel.

The Tariff Commission, in obedience to the commands of the steel interest, was prepared to admit all blooms not less than 5 inches square at 6–10 of one cent a pound, or $13.44 a ton, at present value equal to a duty of 64 per cent. This size can only be used by railmakers. Under present conditions this rate would be as prohibitory as if the rate were $50. The railmakers all make their own steel. All other sizes used by our manufacturing industries the Commission had classified as follows : " Steel ingots, cogged ingots, blooms, etc., etc." (here follows a long list of enumerations), " *less* than 5 inches, valued at 5 cents a pound or less, 2 cents per pound ; valued above 5 cents and not above 9 cents per pound, 2¾ cents per pound ; valued at above 9 cents, 3½ cents per pound." For Bessemer steel in ingots, bars, blooms, billets, etc., there are no such valuations. The Commissioners might as well have said "a dollar or less." Instead of 5 cents a pound or $112 a ton, the values are as follows (in smaller sizes there may be a difference of a few dollars a ton) :

	Value.
Bessemer Ingots	$20
Blooms	. 21
Billets	. 23

TARIFF, PROPOSED BY THE COMMISSION.

On Bessemer Ingots $44 40, equal to, *ad valorem*, . .	222 per cent.
Blooms 44 40, " " . . .	211 per cent.
Billets 44 40, " " . . .	193 per cent.

In order to make no more mistakes, like the one that opened the door to the entry of blooms at a low rate, the steel interest further ordained as follows :

"Provided, that all metal produced from iron or its ores, which is cast and malleable, of whatever description or form, without regard to the percentage of carbon contained therein, whether produced by cementation, or converted, cast, or made from iron or its ores, by the crucible, Bessemer, pneumatic, Thomas Gilchrist, basic, Siemens-Martin, or open-hearth process, or by the equivalent of either, or by the combination of two or more of the processes or their equivalents, or by any fusion or other process which produces from iron or its ores a metal either granular or fibrous in structure, which is cast and malleable, excepting what is known as malleable iron castings, shall be classed and denominated as steel."

"Steel in any form, not specially enumerated or provided for in this act, three cents per pound," $67.20 per ton. The old tariff says : "Steel in any other form not otherwise provided for, 30 per centum *ad valorem*." Thirty per centum on steel not classified raised to 300 per cent.!

The enactment of this marvellously audacious scheme would have ruined all the manufacturers of steel manufactures, machinery, tools, and implements, and made of the Bessemer men one great consolidated monopoly, second only to the Standard Oil Company. The tariff on "manufactures, articles, or wares, composed wholly or in part of iron, steel, etc., was to be 45 per cent. *ad valorem*" against 200 per cent. on steel. The steel ring knew that this scheme could not have been carried without the aid of some other powerful combination in Congress. Such a combination was in fact standing ready in close phalanx to renew the old alliance. The wool-growers were equally desirous to push for more "government subsidy." The bargain found expression in the proposition of the Commission for a slight reduction in the wool schedule, as mentioned in one of the foregoing chapters, but a doubling of rates in washed wools of class No. II and No. III, and a classification of cow's hair, hitherto free, as wool, and the levying of corresponding duties. This was the sop to "the farmer."

The guardians of the interests of the people, the House of Representatives, or rather, the Committee of Ways and Means, under the leadership of Mr. Kelley, made haste to prepare a bill containing all the above enumerated iron-clad provisions. They were all framed by the rings of iron and steel men or their representatives. Vigorous opposition was made in the Senate. Under the able leadership of Mr. Beck, from Kentucky, the scheme was defeated. The new law makes 45 per cent. the rate for all forms of steel under 4 cents a pound. This is virtually more than the old law intended it to be. (The courts have meanwhile decided that 30 per cent. was to be the rate for all blooms imported under appeal.) Considering, however, that the new and definite rate of 45 per cent. solves the long-pending uncertainty, our manufacturers may well be pleased in having escaped the greater danger, at least for the time being.

But even under this new tariff law manufacturers of finished goods in the iron and steel line, machinery, tools, hardware, etc., are in about the same condition in which manufacturers of woollen goods, cloaks, etc., find themselves. Their condition would be greatly improved by absolute free trade. They are protected by a tariff of 45 per cent., but have to pay the following tariff advances on English prices :

On ore, 75 cents a ton,[1] equal to 30 per cent.

Pig-iron pays $6.72, or about 60 per cent.

Bar-iron pays according to size, from $17 to $24.64 a ton, or equal to *ad-valorem* rates of 60 to 75 per cent.

Sheet-iron, $24.64 to $33.60 a ton, or equal to *ad-valorem* rates of 62½ to 75 per cent.

---

[1] This is an advance over the rate of the old tariff, which was 20 per cent. The new tariff law raises this to 75 cents to please Mr. Mahone and a few wealthy mine-owners.

It is quite a phenomenon, that the more our infants mature, the more they need the protecting nurse.

THE AVERAGE INVOICE VALUE OF FOREIGN ORE WAS IN

1872	$2 08, duty 20 per cent.,	41¾ cents.
1873	2 25, "	45 "
1875	2 57, " "	51¼ "
1878	2 14, " "	43 "
1882	2 86, " "	57 "

Forty-one and three-fourth cents was sufficient in 1872 to protect the great industrial skill required in ore-digging. Ten years later, under an advance of foreign ore prices, 57 cents did not protect, and the duty had to be raised to 75 cents. According to the census, nearly two tons of ore were used in the making of a ton of pig-iron, equal to a charge of $1.50 on a ton, instead of $1.14 on the price of 1882, and 83 cents on that of 1872.

Hoop-iron, $22.40 to $31.36 a ton, or equal to *ad-valorem* rates of 65 to 85 per cent.

Copper in plates, bars, Chili pigs, etc., 4 cents a pound, or $89.60 a ton, equal to *ad-valorem* rate of about 30 per cent.

Copper, rolled plates, 35 per cent.

Steel, of all kinds and in any form of less value than 4 cents a pound, 45 per cent.

The reader will see at a glance how much more the manufacturer of metal goods has to pay in mostly all instances for his materials than he gets back in the tariff on manufactures. All of these discriminations against him he has to overcome by superior methods and greater efficiency of labor.

The steel makers are dissatisfied, and will try again undoubtedly. I wish them good-speed, and strength to their elbows. Reforms are usually accelerated more by the unmeasured demands and arrogant presumptions of those enjoying privileges and monopolies than by preachings and appeals to the suffering, apathetic victims.

How well the United States Government has been caring for these "infants," however, in the past, may be seen from this statement of one year's business :

The Bulletin of the American Iron and Steel Association of January, 1880, says :

"In the following table we give the prices at Philadelphia and in Pennsylvania of various iron and steel products on the 1st of January, 1879, and the 1st of January, 1880, with the percentage of increase in the intervening year. The prices are fair average prices : "

ARTICLES.	Jan. 1, 1879.	Jan. 1, 1880.	Per cent. of Increase.
No. 1 anthracite foundry pig-iron in Philadelphia	$17 00	$35 00	106
Best refined bar-iron in Philadelphia . . .	42 56	71 68	68
Bessemer-steel rails at works in Philadelphia .	42 00	70 00	67
Best iron rails in Philadelphia	34 00	57 00	68
Cut nails by the keg in Philadelphia . . .	2 10	4 25	102
Old iron rails in Philadelphia	19 00	36 00	89
No. 1 wrought scrap in Philadelphia . . .	20 00	34 00	70

Assuming that this increase was realized for the product of the mills for the year (from July 1, 1879, to June 30, 1880), then the profits must have been enormous, as may be seen by multiplying the product by the extra price realized over that of 1879. I know very well that the iron and steel men will say that those prices were not realized all through. But considering the enormous demand that followed, and continued increasingly even, we may allow ourselves to believe that that year's product did not fall much short of those prices. The Bulletin goes on to say :

"But the most remarkable fact in connection with the history of the American iron trade of 1879 remains to be stated. Notwithstanding all the activity that has been mentioned, the demand for pig-iron, iron and steel rails, and iron ore was not met, and many orders have been carried over to the new year which consumers sought in vain to have filled in 1879."

It is safe, therefore, to say that the " boom " which animated the iron trade during the whole of the fiscal year of 1880 (the census year) gave the iron and steel mills all the tariff allowed them to charge in excess of the foreign price and freight.

PRODUCT OF MILLS.	Tons.	Duty.	Profit Guaranteed by Tariff.
Pig iron.	3,780,000	7	$25,500,000
Bar and rod iron	808,000	22 40	18,000,000
Plate and sheet iron	532,000	33 60	18,000,000
Iron rails	467,000	15 68	7,500,000
Other products	540,000	22 40	12,000,000
Steel rails, etc.	741,000	28 00	21,000,000
Steel bars, etc.	242,000	50 00	12,000,000
			$114,000,000

This is what the tariff did for the iron and steel men
    in the year of the boom $114,000,000
The wages of 140,978 workingmen were . .   55,476,000

Even allowing for the toll iron and steel manufacturers had to pay to the pig-iron men, it can be safely maintained that to all of those poor stipendiaries and claimants a tariff for the protection of the American workingman proved to be something more than a mere catchword. Of course the medal has a reverse, the same as in the woollen line, over-supply making itself felt as soon as the demand slackens. The iron and steel men, however, had a better opportunity to feather their nests. They had prepared for a rainy day. It is only the workingman who again fared as the Indian did. Said the white hunter : "Here is crow for you and turkey for me, and here is turkey for me and crow for you."

CHAPTER IX.

I here rest my case, so far as "protection of our industries" is concerned, and beg the kind reader to follow me through the chapter : "We are a young nation, and as such cannot compete with the older nations of Europe." This chapter will have no ponderous figures to be worked through. It will be pleasant writing and reading ; for who does not wish to hear from his most formidable rival the acknowledgment of his superiority wherever the intellect is called to play in subduing the inertness of matter ? Let me simply quote unimpeachable authorities :

The Parliament of Great Britain in February, 1750, appointed a commission whose chairman, after a few days of deliberation, brought in a bill which permitted American iron in its rudest form to be imported duty free ; but, now that the nailers in the colonies could afford spikes and large nails cheaper than the English, it forbade the smiths of America to erect any mill for slitting or rolling iron, or any plating-forge to work with a tilt-hammer, or any furnace for making steel. The House divided on the proposal that every slitting mill in America should be abolished. The clause failed by a majority of only twenty-two ; but an immediate return was required of every mill already existing, and the number was never to be increased." (George Bancroft, quoted in Mr. Swank's Report on Iron and Steel.)

This policy was continued by Great Britain up to the time of the War of Independence. It shows what an exalted opinion England had more than a hundred years ago of America and her industries. I may be told in reply that this does not apply to these times, with their thousand-fold increased and improved appliances. Well, we have kept pretty well up to the times. An American will never stand back if you only give him a chance.

I will quote from most recent authorities. *The Engineer*, of London, of the 7th of January, 1881, says :

"The United States iron-masters are beating us by 100 per cent. in the output from their plant. With one pair of converters they can do as much and more than we can do with two pairs ; and, while our blast furnaces turn out 480 tons of pig per week, theirs, much smaller, give as much as 1,100 tons a week. In the rail mills, and bar and steel mills, matters are in much the same condition. If we are asked to what is this superiority due, we reply that it is to be traced, to some extent, to better organization, and in others to better plant. In the Bessemer works, for example, the drill of the men employed is perfect, and a converter is never stopped for days while being lined-up and rebottomed.

"In the United States, for a long time back, the moment a converter is burned out it is taken away, and a new one is put in its place. The operation requires, we understand, about half an hour at the most. In how many English steel works is the same plan pursued ? A great deal of the blast-furnace plant of Great Britain is antiquated, and the sooner it is replaced with more modern plant the better."

This and similar quotations are contained in Mr. Swank's report to the Census Bureau, consequently approved by him. He himself, the Secretary of the Iron and Steel Association of America, consequently unimpeachable protectionist authority, makes the following statements as to the efficiency of American iron- and steel-makers :

"Although this country cannot produce iron and steel as cheaply as European countries which possess the advantages of cheap labor and proximity of raw materials, it is not excelled by any other country in the skill which it displays, or the mechanical and scientific economies which it practises in any branch of their manufactures, while in certain leading branches it has displayed superior skill and shown superior aptitude for economical improvements. Our blast-furnace practice is the best in the world.

"The excellent quality of our pig-iron is universally conceded. Our Bessemer-steel practice is also the best in the world. We produce much more Bessemer-steel rails in a given time by a given amount of machinery, technically termed a plant, than any of our European rivals.

" All of our leading iron and steel works, and indeed many of our small works, are now supplied with systematic chemical investigations by their own chemists, who are often men of eminence in their profession. The managers of our blast furnaces, rolling-mills, and steel-works, are themselves frequently well-educated chemists, metallurgists, geologists, or mechanical engineers, and sometimes all of these combined. Our rapid progress in increasing our production of iron and steel is not merely the result of good fortune or the possession of unlimited natural resources, but is largely due to the possession of accurate technical knowledge by our iron-masters, and by those who are in charge of their works, combined with the characteristic American dash which all the world has learned to respect and to admire."

What is said here of iron and steel manufacture may be said of most of our leading industries. As to cotton goods, State Department Report No. 12, " Commercial Relations of the United States," page 98, says :

" Undoubtedly, the inequalities in the wages of English and American operatives are more than equalized by the greater efficiency of the latter and their longer hours of labor. If this should prove to be a fact in practice, as it seems to be proven from official statistics, it would be a very important element in the establishment of our ability to compete with England for our share of the cotton-goods trade of the world."

The report of the Chief of the Massachusetts Bureau of Statistics of Labor, Mr. Carroll D. Wright, shows that all the testimony he has taken and published in Public Document No. 15 establishes that our mills have higher speed and better organization than the English mills, and that more goods are turned out in ten hours than formerly in eleven. Says one spinner : " Speed is an absolute science in Fall River, and what the superintendents and overseers do not know about it, you may rest assured is not worth knowing." Another : " When we used to run eleven hours we got off 100 pounds less than we do now with ten hours." And still another : " I have been nine years in Fall River, and have never worked anywhere else, except in England, where we worked at high speed, but not to the extent practised here."

The silk industry has found its development in this country

later than any of the above mentioned. Hear what the Secretary of the Silk Association of America says about this industry :

"Our manufacturers have been obliged, on the contrary, to concentrate the work, so as to keep every portion of it under direct supervision. In several of our larger silk-mills all the different processes referred to are conducted beneath a single roof, so that the raw silk becomes finished goods under the eye of the manufacturer. In some instances these mills have within their walls rooms provided with all tools and machinery for their own repairing and carpentering work ; a few make nearly all their machines. There is a marked disposition to try improvements in this country, and it is the general experience that the very best machinery, though at first far more costly, is in the end decidedly the cheapest. It seems evident, however, that the division of the processes between three or four separate establishments [speaking of European methods]—throwsters, dyers, weavers, and probably finishers—must imply an added cost in a profit to each. The American system is largely a consequence of substituting machinery for manual labor. The work of the power-loom is definite and positive ; it is not liable to defects such as happen to hand-made goods if the weaver's hand is unsteady in throwing the shuttle, or if he is careless in using the number of picks required by the patterns." •

From all sides we hear anxious inquiries about the stoppage of demand from America, where one line after another of foreign silks is supplanted by the products of American power-looms. American silk machinery is exported to districts where the industry has had a home for generations. If we are still crowded from our own markets by foreign, excessively taxed silks, it is not so much on account of higher labor rates, but because our protected industries neglect to follow up the progress of foreign industries in manipulation and the use of substitute materials.

China-grass under special treatment presents characteristics scarcely inferior to silk. If mixed with silk the best judges of silks are often misled.

The consular reports to the State Department and American trade journals[1] have called attention to the extensive use of substi-

---

[1] The New York Dry Goods Bulletin has very systematically followed up all the recent developments of the new industry.

tutes in silks and woollens in European countries. Here very little progress has been made in investigation and application. It is not foreign to all our manufacturers, however, and I am told that those using it are doing so with great profit to themselves, while others complain of their inability to compete with foreign makes.

It is evident from this that the tariff, that great providential power, cannot guarantee success and protection against the foreigner if our manufacturers do not use their brain power against him. They surely have always a great stock of this commodity in store when it is to be used to hunt down their own countrymen and competitors, in which warfare they use the scalping-knife in true Modoc fashion.

Regarding the character of our help and wages as affecting prices, I will conclude the introduction of authorities with extracts from the statement of Mr. Joseph D. Weeks, Expert and Special Agent of the Census, made to Mr. Joseph. Nimmo, Chief of the Bureau of Statistics, Washington, D. C., May 22, 1882 :

" I do not mean to say that, man for man, naturally the American workingman in the iron mills is better than the Englishman. I simply mean to say that he is willing to work more and harder, and consequently turns out a great deal more product. For example, a case in question has just come to my notice. The iron-workers in the north of England have just made a demand for 7½ per cent. advance, and for what they term 'prize money,' this prize money being what we would call extra for over-time and holidays, or an extra price paid for working at unusual times, at night or Sunday. Now, they claim that Monday should be regarded as a holiday, and refuse to work Monday unless they are paid an extra price for doing so. If they should work Monday they would probably turn out as much as any other day ; but by their system of working, Monday being regarded as a holiday and Saturday as a half-holiday, they lose more time than the American does ; consequently their effectiveness is less. It does not affect the general statement, however, if the word 'effectiveness' is properly construed. We also say 'while wages per ton in many cases are nearly the same, the earnings per diem are fully twice as much,' with the same consideration that this does not mean a day that an American would work as hard as he could, but per day for a number of consecutive days, say for six months. There is no trouble about that statement either."

All of the above testimony ought to be sufficient to prove that we have reached maturity, that our industries have passed the stage of infancy, and that the people of the United States may justly demand to be treated by their law-makers with the consideration which is due to full-grown rational men—beings endowed with reason.

CHAPTER X.

Unnecessary stress is usually laid upon the higher or lower rate of wages ruling in this or in that country. As an argument in tariff agitation, it is of no value whatsoever. It is certain that wages are not gauged by protective legislation, but by demand and supply ; or, in other words, the general opportunities of the country, which, in their turn, determine the general mode of living. Wherever these agencies are of the highest, there wages are highest. Wherever they are highest, there production is the highest and products are cheapest. Apparently a paradox, but it is true nevertheless.

High wages foster invention, and that country has ever done most in this realm of thought whose people are used to a higher mode of living. Buckle's theory of the principal causes that influence civilization, viz., food, soil, climate, and the general aspect of nature, is fully corroborated in its application to industrial development.

Food, soil, climate, and the general aspect of nature are more potent in determining the relative conditions of nations in the world's contest for supremacy than all the enactments of paternal governments. Nay, more ; wherever they favor a nation preeminently above others they are potent enough to overcome many of the injuries which the stupidity of law-makers has heaped upon a people for generations. No country possesses all these natural advantages to a greater extent than the United States. Unlimited in their food supply, the people of the United States owe it solely to the above-mentioned quality of their legislators if there is want in the midst of abundance; but, on the whole, no better-fed people exists than ours. Scratch the soil and it brings forth fruit, unmanured and with far less labor than elsewhere. Indeed we have not arrived even at the beginning of a rational system of agriculture.

59

Climate ? The very air throughout the widest stretch of the land invites to vigorous activity. The veriest clod imported from the Old World takes hold of his hoe, his axe, his hammer, or his chisel, in a way entirely new to him, as soon as the strangeness of the thing has worn off ; and I doubt whether it is any thing else than the nerve that is imparted by the climate that makes such good Americans of such raw material in so short a time. The general aspect of nature is certainly all that can be required. And with all these natural advantages so liberally supplied to us, can it be that we require protection ? Protection against those who are weaker than we ? The young, the healthy, the strong, against the old, the sick, the weak, soldier-ridden, and oppressed peoples of Europe ? The very thought is an absurdity.

The application of labor-saving machinery driven by steam and other elementary power, has wrought a revolution in economics, which fact has not yet been sufficiently recognized by our lawmakers. Where labor is degraded to the lowest possible level, the introduction of these agencies is hardly ever thought of. The lowness of wages makes it possible to dispense with the putting up of high-cost plant, buildings, and machinery, and the consequent interest charges and expenses. Contrariwise, labor can never be so poorly paid where a large number of workmen are collected under one roof or in one town. They can combine, and do combine to resist reduction in wages. Manufacturers, possessors of large fixed capital, if they can see ever so slight a profit in running their mill, will hesitate to run the risk of a strike. This is not so with those industries where the work is divided all over the towns and the country districts among a great number of small masters and workpeople. The so-called house-industries of Germany and other countries, despite incredibly low wages, find themselves frequently crowded from their markets by American competition, and by the fruit of high-cost organization. To illustrate : The manufacture of slates has been an old-established industry in Thuringia, and is one of the hardest, unhealthiest, and most poorly paid occupations. The family composes the workshop. Women—wife and daughters—carry the stone from the quarry to the shop in loads of from 100 to 125 pounds. In winter, while so burdened, the steam rises from them visibly ; panting as they do for breath, you hear them at a distance. To take a short rest from their exertion, they sit down in the snow, and most of them are troubled with lung diseases, and die an early death. The men are equally hard at work, equally exposed in cold, draughty huts. Besides, they inhale the dust and leady coloring matter; and with all this slaving the *combined* efforts and toiling do not realize more than a few marks, or fifty cents a day. They use the old methods and tools of a hundred years ago. Now they complain of harder times yet; America, formerly a very great market for their hand-made slates, has not only ceased to buy, but with her machine-made slates, superior in make and finish and beauty, is beginning to compete seriously with them in their home market, Germany.

There are villages in the Taunus, within an hour's walk from Frankfort-on-the-Main, a city noted for having more millionnaires within its walls than any other city of the world, considering its size, where nail-making is one of the long-developed home industries. A strong nail-maker can earn about 1.25 mark, or 30 cents, by a day's work of twelve hours. Wire-making yields to an equally industrious worker 1.35 to 1.65 mark (32½ to 40 cents). Of course women and children are equally pressed to work—children only part of their time. Filet work, knitting or embroidering work, yields to an expert hand about 50 to 55 pfennige, or 12 to 14 cents. Children of the tenderest age are kept steadily at work, from early dawn and often till midnight, with only such intermissions as school-time and the satisfaction of bodily wants compel. Some, if ever so steady at their filet-needles. do not earn more than 25 pfennige, or 6 cents, as a long day's wages. The family may be called happy whose average daily income during the year does not fall below 2 marks, or fifty cents, a day. Working hours are from 5 A.M. to 7 P.M., winter and summer alike. The nail-maker carries his own goods to market, the same as his ancestors did hundreds of years ago.

I have before me a statement of the earnings of a large family, composed of father, mother, two sons,—the father's helpers in nail-making,—and three daughters,—filet work and knitting— six workers (not counting the mother), earning all told about 1,400 marks, or $350. Deducting Sundays, which, however, does not re- lieve the girls entirely, and counting only 300 work days, brings

The father's earnings at 40 cents	.	.	.	$120
" 2 sons' " " 25 " each	.	.	150
" 3 daughters' " " 10 " "	.	.	90
					$360

From the reports of the factory inspectors it appears that the handloom weavers' earnings are even below those of the Taunus nail-makers. The yearly income of a weaver in the Silesian mountain districts is not above three hundred marks, or $75. A patch of land to grow potatoes is all he has to help him in bridging over the abyss of misery that lies hidden beneath such scanty earnings, and a year of misgrowth often means starvation and death to him and his family.

Compared to such low earnings, those of the nail-makers of the Black Country of England may be called liberal pay. Yet they are low enough compared to the wages of factory hands. I take my figures from a recent letter written in the protectionist interest to the *New York Tribune.* It says :

"An expert nailer, working steadily from Monday morning to Friday night [5 days, against the 6 overworked days of the German nail-maker], can only make two and a half bundles of iron rods into nails, for which he gets 6s. 7½d. per bundle, or, for his week's work, 16s. 8d., exactly four dollars. Now his wife, by working every moment of her spare time and late into the night—neglecting her wretched little children—can make a bundle of commoner nails, for which she is paid 3s. 1d., and the little half-starved, stunted girl of twelve, with her brown arms and steady, unerring aim, will hammer out half a bundle, 1s. 6½d. Total earnings of an industrious and hard-working family, three at the forge, for the entire week :

	English Money.	United States Money.
Father	16s. 8d.	$4 00
Mother	3s. 1d.	74
Daughter	1s. 7½d.	39
Total gross earnings of the family per week . .	21s. 4½d.	$5 13

"But out of this pittance must come 3d. for carriage of iron from the 'fogger's' and returning the nails, 1s. for the smithy fire, and 3d. for the wear of tools. Net earning, $4.77 per week —the united earnings of three industrious, sober persons."

The results of the different methods are significant. In the Taunus, near Frankfort, the raw material in a thousand horseshoe nails—

No. 8 costs 35 cents ; wages, 32¼ ; percentage of wages to material, 93
" 6 " 26 " " 26 ; " " " " 100

or an average of 96¼ %

Nail-making in the United States consumes in raw material, exclusive of fuel, $2,800,000. The wages of the 2,900 persons employed amounts to $1,255,000, or $410 for each hand ; or, at 300 days, 1 36⅔ cents a day. Thus, in the American method, labor constitutes only 31½ per cent. of nail-making, exclusive of profits, and yields 1 36⅔ cents to the workman, while the house industry requires 50 per cent. of the product (also excluding profits) for a day's wages of barely 30 cents. The result is :—

American method, nails, 100; material, 68¼; labor, 31¾; wages, $1 36¼.
German " " 100; " 51; " 49; " 30.

Though the earnings of an American are 4½ times higher than those of his German fellow-workman, yet his wages compose only 31½ per cent. of the product, while under the German method they are 49 per cent. of the product. In other words, the labor-cost in American-made goods is about 35 per cent. less, while the earnings of the laborer are 350 per cent. more, than under the old methods.

In English manufactures—like the hosiery, knit-goods, some woollen and silk industries—we find the same rule prevailing, lower wages and earnings wherever the hand-loom and knitting-frame give employment to small masters in their own houses and homes. But such a system of work hardly exists in America, and where it does exist, it is being rapidly extinguished by the power-mill—which, in turn, not only offers serious competition to Germany and England, but is duly recognized by them as their great impending danger.

Now, I do not wish the reader to suppose that these low earnings of those engaged in house-industries are of recent date. The English and German statements, even previous to 1845, paint blacker yet. It is not my task at present to write a history of white slavery in the present century, but simply to point out the utter invalidity of such irrelevant comparisons as our protectionist agitators are in the habit of exhibiting,—comparisons of things that are as dissimilar as the moon and a green cheese.

But even where the product of our power-machinery meets their power-mill product the same holds good.

It costs less in New England and Pennsylvania to spin and weave a pound of cotton into cloth than in Old England, though the weekly earnings of our people are higher. This statement is best supported by a reference to the annual consumption of pounds of cotton by each hand employed in the industry in the leading countries:

	Pounds cotton used.	Number hands employed.	Pounds consumed per hand employed.
United States	750,343,000	172,544	4,337
Great Britain	1,471,357,000	482,903	3,253
Germany	300,000,000	250,000	1,200

(The same relationship exists in other branches, and in the application of steam- and other power-engines.)[1]

This advantage on our side is more than lost by the taxes and interest charges on the high cost of the plant and mill, the high cost of coal and other materials, all heavily taxed, which, all combined, outweigh by nearly two cents on the pound the saving in the cost of labor before alluded to. English hands, on the other side, in fifty-six hours, earn on the average about one-fourth more than French mill-hands in seventy-two hours. Yet the cost of the manufacture of a kilogram of cotton yarn is 9.6 cents in England against 15.6 in France. The items are as follow:

[1] For 1875 the steam-engines used in the various industries of England are given at 936,405 horse power. For 1880 the steam-engines used in the various industries of the United States are given at 2,185,458.

	France.	England.
Labor	0.054	0.043
Expenses	0.056	0.022
Interest, etc.	0.046	0.031
	0.156	0.096

Italy stands worse yet in the scale. I could bring forward similar statistical proof against the other nations I have spoken of, but it would be only a repetition of items. But why go across the ocean? We find the same conditions and results in our own country.

I have made a classification of the yearly earnings of our cotton and woollen operatives in the different sections of the country. In woollens they are as follows :

Connecticut	. . . \$335	New York.	. . . \$285
Maine	. . . 320	New Hampshire	. . 280
Massachusetts	. . 320	Vermont	. . . 270
Pennsylvania	. . 300	Indiana	. . . 230
New Jersey	. . 300	Ohio.	. . . 196

In cotton industries they are as follows :

Maine . .		New York.	. . . \$218
New Hampshire	. . \$255	South Carolina .	. . 190
New Jersey .		Maryland .	. . . 188
Massachusetts	. . 251	Georgia	. . . 180
Rhode Island	. . 250	Tennessee.	. . . 160
Pennsylvania	. . 250	Alabama .	. . . 160
Ohio . .	. . 250	Virginia	. . . 150
Connecticut	. . 242	North Carolina .	. . 135

If cheap, or rather low-priced, labor determines superiority in productive capacity, why does not the South drive the New England and Middle States from the field and flood us with cheap fabrics? Why does not the West, New York, or New Jersey supersede Connecticut, Maine, and Massachusetts in woollens? But take our own city, with its varied manufacturing enterprises, most of which have little if any protection against Europe, and none against our inland competing cities. Most of the materials that enter into New York's industries are so highly protected, that this tax in many cases outweighs even the very high tax on the finished goods. Still New York manufactures more goods than the New England States, if we except Massachusetts. Our manufactures are $470,000,000, or nearly ten per cent. of all the manufacturing industries of the whole country. Most of them are goods of the highest finish, in which New York is the leading centre. New York pays the highest wages. In comparison with Philadelphia wages, I find in nearly fifty items differences ranging from twenty-five to fifty per cent. in the yearly earnings of New York's working classes above those of Philadelphia. And still New York manages to get along, and exceeds Philadelphia's annual production of $324,000,000 by $150,000,000, or nearly 50 per cent.

The highest wage-earners make the best goods ; and while these always find a ready market, the cheap stuff of so many of our mills is, as at present, a drug in the market, breeding ruin all around.

I believe after the testimony introduced, that I need not fear contradiction when I state that our mode of manufacture is not only fully equal, but in most instances superior, to that of the most advanced commercial nations of the globe. I can therefore advance a few closing remarks in reference to that great protectionist argument : *American labor must be protected against the starvation wages of Europe.* In view of the fact that all our protected industries are making the most extensive use of free trade in labor, this point seems rather frivolous. Yet greatest stress is laid by our orators upon this very point. Not only on the Fourth of July, but on all other state occasions ; at all political performances, wherever and whenever the Honorable the member from Buncombe finds a fit opportunity, there and then great show is made of his solicitude for the protection of American labor. The Commissioner of Labor of the State of Massachusetts some years ago commented on the displacement of one class of labor in factories by another. This process has continued to this day, the cheaper always replacing the dearer labor ; the American, the English, the German, the Irish, the French Canadian, and finally the Scandinavian, all in turn making sacrifice to the corporation. In other words, competition for the cheapest mode of production is so keen that manufacturers are always endeavoring to replace labor that has become accustomed to American life and mode of living

by labor that has been trained to a cheaper standard. All nation-
alities and races, however, share alike in the endeavor to improve
their condition, to strive for the highest wages ruling in the
country, and to maintain the standard of living once gained. So
uncontrovertible a truth is this, that hardly any thing need be
said in its support. Yet so brilliant an illustration has come
to my notice that I cannot refrain from mentioning it. A Chinese
shoe manufacturing firm in San Francisco, employing Chinese
laborers, gave their workmen their daily meals at the factory, for
which they were charged 50 cents a day. After a time the men
demanded that their meals be furnished gratis whenever work
should be slack and they earn no wages. This the firm refused to
their countrymen and the Chinese struck work. White men, new
arrivals, were put in their places, ready to work for wages which
the despised Mongolians had refused to accept. I merely bring
this in as evidence that wages are not gauged in this country on
sentimental principles, as our protectionists would have us believe,
but that, protected or not protected, our manufacturers try to obtain the cheapest labor wherever they can get it, which endeavor
the workingman will resist as long as possible, and if unsuccessful
he will always strive to regain his former standard of living whenever opportunity favors him. The high-wages standard can be
maintained without detriment to manufactures, as is shown above,
and besides is of a great advantage in another direction.

The laborer is the great consumer of commodities ; consequently
well-paid labor sustains business prosperity. If the workingman
does not earn fair wages, every thing comes to a standstill. Hence
the cutting-down process eventually recoils on those who are the
innocent or guilty cause of it. Nor even does the high-wage
country suffer from the low wages of competing countries. The
poor, wretched linen-weavers of Silesia—a class of whom it can
hardly be said that any one of them has ever had a full square
meal of butcher's meat, and among whom hunger-typhus (typhus
caused by starvation) is a calamity of frequent recurrence—earn
about half of the not over-paid weavers of Belfast. Yet the markets of unprotected England are only flooded to the extent of
£20,000 of German linen a year. One of our best authorities in
political economy, Mr. Edward Atkinson, stated the case very

forcibly in a letter to Mr. Nimmo, the Chief of the Bureau of Statistics at Washington. I cannot do better than close this chapter by quoting his remarks bearing on this point :

" Further, the use of machinery, and the cost of the production of such machinery, depend upon the intelligence, manual skill, and physical ability of the operative who directs it. Most of the work being done by the piece, the operative who earns the highest wages working on piece-work produces cloth at the lowest cost.

" When all these elements are taken into consideration, I think it follows that any one who attempts to gauge the cost of production by comparison of wages will most likely be misled ; and if it is assumed that the lowest cost of production will be found where the wages are lowest, he will be sure to be misled, as that rule would lead to the expectation of finding the lowest cost of cotton fabrics in the factories of India ; next in the factories of Germany ; next, perhaps, of France ; and last, perhaps, of England ; the upward sequence of wages being substantially according to the order named.

" We have about 175,000 persons in our cotton factories, of whom about 160,000 work for the home market. By comparing the product of the hand-carders, spinners, and weavers who were at Atlanta, I gauged their capacity, and I found that if we still depended on that method, about 16,000,000 of our population would be needed to make our present supply in place of 160,000 now at work.

" The capacity of an operative directing our modern automatic machinery being one hundred-fold that of an operative working the hand-card, wheel, and hand-loom ; assuming that our adult faculty operatives earn about one dollar a day each, it follows that the successful competitor on hand-worked machinery would need to work at one cent a day in order to compete.

" Apply this rule to the Chinese, the largest body of people using cotton in the world, and mostly clothed by hand-made goods. It will be apparent that it would be fallacious to compute or to infer a low cost of manufacture because Chinese wages are low. If we then take the two extremes of the operatives working by hand on machinery in China, and the operative directing modern machinery in Lowell, we find that in Lowell, where the high relative wages are paid, the low relative cost is to be found.

" Hence follows this rule : *Other things being equal, high wages coupled with low cost are the necessary result of the most intelligent application of machinery to the arts, provided the education of the operative keeps pace with the improvement of the machinery.*

" This fundamental principle must be comprehended in order that any valuable deductions may be made from wages ; and before the true cost of any fabric can be determined, the *other things* which are not equal must be ascertained."

CHAPTER XI.

We need not fear foreign competition, even if our labor be better paid than labor is paid in Europe, were we to go to work at once and reform the tariff, first, by freeing raw materials, and secondly, by reducing correspondingly all duties on manufactured goods. In order, however, to convince all sincere friends of the workingman that the latter is not protected by the tariff, I will show what his earnings are in reality, what they are in excess of his former earnings under a low tariff, and, finally, how far he is ahead of the best-paid European labor—the English—his principal rival. Thus it will be seen what amount of duty would have to be levied to protect his interests, and that these could be well taken care of under a revenue tariff.

A most essential feature in the estimate of wages is the cost of living. To compute wages by the dollar sign is as erroneous and as difficult as to calculate the Copernican from the Ptolemaic system ; a changeable value to pay for a fixed value. A changeable value—buying more in one country than in another—changeable as to time in the same country—is not a true measure for a fixed value, that of the working day or of the cost of living of the laborer. This change in the value of the dollar (or any other money) causes the perturbations of which our present strikes are the logical outgrowth. The value of our own dollar during the various periods of protection, taking as a basis 1860 and proceeding to our present time, has been compiled by Mr. Carroll D. Wright :

WHAT ONE DOLLAR COULD BUY IN

					1860.	1872.	1878.	1881.
Flour, superfine	.	.	.	. lbs.	25.64	18.18	22.72	19.76
Codfish	.	.	.	"	18.87	12.20	16.67	13.33
Beans .	.	.	.	"	12.66	10.52	12.05	7.54
Coffee .	.	.	.	"	4.36	2.35	3.77	3.47
Sugar .	.	.	.	"	9.70	8.33	10.00	9.09
Soap .	.	.	.	"	11.49	12.50	12.34	14.81
Beef, roasting	.	.	.	"	9.18	5.26	6.94	5.88
" soup .	.	.	.	"	20.83	13.33	18.86	18.18
" corned	.	.	.	"	15.38	9.52	12.34	9.75
Veal, hindquarters	.	.	.	"	9.18	5.85	6.53	6.34
Mutton, forequarters	.	.	.	"	13.51	9.80	9.70	8.82
Hams .	.	.	.	"	7.75	7.41	8.07	6.55
Potatoes	.	.	.	bushels	1.67	0.97	1.03	0.79
Milk .	.	.	.	quarts	21.27	12.50	18.86	16.66
Coal .	.	.	.	. lbs.	312.00	217.00	310.00	255.00
Shirting, 4–4	.	.	.	yards	10.87	7.69	13.33	11.42
Sheeting .	.	.	.	"	9.34	7.14	11.11	9.30
Rent, four-room tenement	.	.	. days	6.75	2.03	5.40	3.75
Board, men .	.	.	.	"	2.51	1.24	1.67	1.47
" women	.	.	.	"	3.92	1.87	2.63	2.33

The money value is changed here all through the list, and the
dollar does not buy the same amount of goods, board, or rent at
any two of the periods.

Cotton goods are about the only things not changed. All other
commodities, but soap, rose in price between 1860 and 1881. Rent
and board about 40 per cent.; potatoes over 50 per cent.; other
victuals from 20 to 40 per centum. The average of prices is
fully one third above the one of the low-tariff period previous
to the war.

Now poor business presses down prices, and wages are reduced.
Good times raise prices, but wages are seldom raised with the rise
of the price of commodities. In most cases their rise has to be
forced : consequently less consumption ensues and strikes follow
in order to regain the former standard of living. 1860 is a year of
a low tariff ; in 1861, prices are beginning to rise greatly in consequence of tariff charges. See the result in consumption per capita :

	Tea. Pounds.	Coffee. Pounds.	Sugar Pounds.	Cereals. Bushels.
1860	0.84	5.8	29.6	38.68
1861	0.52	4.3	22.2	
1862	0.71	3.4	29.5	26.42
1863	0.80	2.2	18.9	21.21
1864 [1]	1.04	3.7	19.4	25.34
1865	0.48	2.8	16.8	31.43
1866	1.16	4.7	27.6	36.67

The slightest change in the value of money falls most severely on the poorer classes. A rise in prices pinches them to that extent that they at once are compelled to reduce their daily rations in tea, coffee, sugar, and *bread*. These few figures tell more than volumes of argument against the fallacy of the attempt to raise the workingman's condition by raising prices through tariff legislation. By the use of such arguments cruel deception is practised.

In justice I will say that in regard to wage matters, "infants" do not differ very materially from "adults." Both as a rule resist a rise in wages so long as compatible with their interests. "Infant" industries, however, are more tenacious, as a rule, in resisting just demands for a rise in wages. The only really protected industries are those of raw materials and crude manufactures. The finer-finish and skill-requiring industries are unprotected, as the taxed material, as a rule, is so high, that all protection-device disappears before the great cost of materials; consequently, by a queer misnomer invented by the sophists of protection, the crude manufactures more than a hundred years old—industries as old as the settlement of any country, ore-digging, metal-smelting, wool-shearing,[2] and kindred skilful manipulations—are the infants of the

[1] 1864 shows heavy importations on account of new duties laid on tea, which, however, are balanced by the lighter imports of 1865. The two years have to be averaged on this account to give a correct estimate of per capita consumption.

[2] As to the kind of labor employed in sheep-raising an expert correspondent to one of our daily papers, gives the following graphic description from one of the far Western sheep-ranges: The business of herding sheep is the most monotonous known. I can imagine no more mind-destroying occupation. It is fit only for greasers, men who are below their dogs in intelligence. It is seldom an American engages in sheep herding. When hard up and unable to obtain other work they wisely prefer the penitentiary and its mild excitement to prowling over a desert after a flock of stupid sheep, and they are right. I have seen sheep herders in Southern Colorado sit for hours on a rock or under a sage

nation, while all the newer and more developed industries remain unnoticed. The gray-headed infants will remain infants and plead for all the assistance requisite to tender years so long as the nation remains simple-minded enough to be mystified by such shallow pretence and mimicry.

A repression in the standard of living through a rise in prices of commodities, caused by tariff legislation, inflation of currency or similar causes, is more lasting and more dangerous than one caused by reduction through the process of cutting down in wages. The latter is a known, visible quantity, often resisted to the bitter end. If they have to yield, the workmen usually regain their lost ground at the first return of a demand for labor. The former, however, is a subtle poison, eating into every morsel of food and every shred of clothing, narrowing the rooms in which they live and thus poisoning the air which they breathe. They do not observe this slowly creeping process of decomposition. The money value of their wages is the same, even somewhat higher than before—but alas!—how are they, in their untutored minds, to explain to themselves the cause of the insufficiency, the decline, of their purchasing power. Years of suffering and strife only bring back the former standard. This can be seen from a glance at prices and wages of pig-iron from 1863 to 1865, when manufacturers' profits were enormously high and wages could hardly buy bread enough to fill the hungry stomachs.

The bureau of statistics is authority for the following figures :

YEAR.	Cost of Pig-Iron.	Sales Price.	Cost of Labor Per Ton.
1863	$16 53	$33 00	$2 07
1864	20 97	45 00	2 85
1865	32 21	60 00	4 56

Will any one be surprised that the consumption of the most indispensable necessities of life had within these years to undergo so marked a decrease as shown above ?

brush looking at a flock of sheep, or slowly walking to and fro in the dust rising behind the animals as they fed over the prairie. These men led a life of such irritating monotony that a nervous American, forced to do the work, would have swallowed one of the banana-like cactuses growing on the plains, in his mad desire to break the direful monotony.

The rapid rise in the price of commodities and the very slow and inadequate rise in wages are sufficient explanation.

Consequently, any legislation tending to raise prices above their normal standard is oppression practised on the people, of whom more than nine tenths are either workingmen, small farmers, or people of small incomes.

The tax on raw materials in wool, iron, coal, dye-stuffs, etc., especially increases the prices of manufactures disproportionately, consequently makes the workingman's dollar less valuable. This may be seen from the following table. Take a pound of scoured wool, for instance, and follow it up until it goes into the possession of the workingman.

UNDER FREE RAW MATERIAL.

Different Processes.	Cost.	Duty.	Labor.	Chemicals and Minerals.	Chem. duty.	Increased cost of Production.	Profit.	Product.
a Scoured wool	$0 50	. .	. .	. .	. .	. .	. .	$0 50
b Wool-dealers' profit	50	. .	. .	. .	. .	. .	$0 05	55
c Cloth price and duties	55	. .	$0 25	$0 25	. .	. .	25	1 30
d Selling expenses and charges	1 30	. .	. .	. .	. .	. .	12	1 42
e Clothing manufacturer	1 42	. .	. .	. .	. .	. .	28	1 70
f Clothing dealer	1 70	. .	. .	. .	. .	. .	42	2 12

UNDER OUR NEW TARIFF ON RAW MATERIALS.

Different Processes.	Cost.	Duty.	Labor.	Chemicals and Minerals.	Chem. duty.	Increased cost of Production.	Profit.	Product.
a Scoured wool	$0 50	30	. .	. .	. .	. .	. .	80
b Wool-dealers' profits	80	. .	. .	. .	. .	. .	10	90
c Cloth price and duties	90	. .	25	25	10	10	40	2 00
d Selling expenses and charges	2 00	. .	. .	. .	. .	. .	20	2 20
e Clothing manufacturer	2 20	. .	. .	. .	. .	. .	45	2 65
f Clothing dealer	2 65	. .	. .	. .	. .	. .	65	3 30

I have allowed under both systems the same percentage of profits to the manufacturers and dealers, and still under protection the workingman has to pay out of his wages for every pound of wool and other protected raw materials, necessary in the process of turning the wool into cloth, even under the revised tariff, $1.18 more than if raw materials were not taxed. The fifty cents' worth of wool and twenty-five cents' worth of chemicals, coal, etc., cost him $1.93 instead of seventy-five cents, the original price ; all on account of the various charges and profits on the tax which the raw material has to bear in its various stages of manufacture until it goes on the workingman's back as a coat. In other words, the tariff charges of forty cents have grown to $1.18,—an increase of seventy-eight cents, in this wonderful process of the tariff to cheapen prices by means of a tax on the raw material.

Prices were fully twenty-five per cent. higher on the average in 1880 than in 1860, while living expenses on the whole—on account of higher prices of commodities and of greater additions to life's necessities—were fully thirty-five per cent. advanced.

Let us examine what were the earnings of our working classes in 1860 and what they were in 1880 in our most important industries. I compute them from the respective census reports by dividing the whole number of persons employed during the year by the total amount of wages paid. The earnings are for the year per head :

	1860.	1880.	Per cent. Increase.
Woollen and worsted goods	$234	$300	28
Iron and steel	355	390	10
Cotton	200	246	23
Machinery	390	450	15
Paper-making	252	360	40
Boots and shoes	250	370	48
Furniture	330	400	20
Sole leather	310	400	28
Glass	330	375	15
Jewelry	435	500	15
Saddlery and harness	350	380	9
Sash and doors	371	400	8

Iron and steel, which, we are told, need so large a protection to keep foreign competition off our shores, though protected by distance, in the shape of charges for transportation, etc., at the rate of from $5 to $7 respectively a ton, have only ten per cent. more to give to the workingman in 1880—a year of unexampled prosperity—than in 1860.

Machinery gave only fifteen per cent., which is about the average of increase in the various lines named above, except in boots and shoes and clothing, where the average increase is forty-eight per cent. owing in great part undoubtedly to the introduction of machinery in place of low-priced hand work, and not to the tariff, as in both instances there is virtually no protection, since the materials were as highly taxed as the finished article.

Considering the smaller purchasing power of the dollar, the workingman received absolutely less wages in the iron and steel mills in 1880 than in 1860. In 1880 the tariff was from fifty to two hundred per cent.; in 1860 twelve per cent. on steel, and twenty-four per cent. on iron.

We have seen above what a good thing the tariff gave to the iron men in 1880, and yet the value of the earnings of their workingmen was considerably less than under the low tariff of 1860. Many of the above enumerated industries did not fare much better. Coal-mining does not,—also one of the " infants," protected by seventy-five cents a ton, or more than fifty per cent. on the cost of production.

In 1880 there were employed :

	Men.	Boys under 16 years.
Above ground	15,564	11,921
Below ground	36,952	3,802

Nearly one fourth of all employed were children. Compared to 1870, the case stood as follows :

	1870.	1880.	Prop. of Inc. p. ct.
Men	43,800	52,500	20
Boys under 16	9,000	15,700	73

Parents, in order to make both ends meet, had to send their children into the mines—thirty per cent. of all employed in 1880 against twenty per cent. in 1870. The output in 1870 was fifteen and a half million tons of anthracite coal, against twenty-seven and a half million tons in 1880. Yet the amount paid in wages was $1,218,000 less in 1880 than in 1870. The tariff for protection of American labor did not prevent the pinching that this decline in wages entailed on our hardest-worked population. What a useful thing an accommodating phrase sometimes proves to be! The earnings of an adult miner in the boom year were $359.08 ; the average of all labor employed in coal mines, $318.

CHAPTER XII.

COMPARING AMERICAN WAGES WITH ENGLISH WAGES, AND SHOW-ING HOW SMALL THE DIFFERENCE IN THE PAY, AND HOW SMALL A TARIFF WOULD BE NEEDED TO PROTECT AMERICAN LABOR, IF RAW MATERIALS WERE FREE.

The superiority of our means of production being acknowledged, little remains to be said to demonstrate that our industries need no protection to enable them to compete successfully with Europe, provided they share the advantages that Europe,—*i. e.*, England, Germany, etc.—possesses ; namely, free raw materials. Our exports in cotton goods are sufficient evidence of this. The same may be said of articles where the skill of the workman, the inventive genius of the American, comes into action. In fact, wherever the value of the work bears a very high relation to the value of the raw material, there we can freely compete with foreign nations. It is so in the case of machinery, tools, implements of all sorts made of iron and steel. Though they are made of materials taxed more heavily than the finished goods, yet the superiority of American workmanship is able to overcome these burdens. Wherever labor largely preponderates in the combined value of labor and materials, there we excel. Of course, in heavy goods, requiring little skill and labor, whose value lies chiefly in the material, competition is altogether out of the question. This alone ought to prove conclusively that though we pay in most fields better wages than even the English—and they pay the highest wages in Europe,—we still make goods that can fully compete with theirs.

We may consider, therefore, a protective tariff, such as we enjoy, as an absolute superfluity that does not benefit the working-man (on the contrary, does him harm in lessening the value of his wages), cripples the manufacturer in narrowing his field of operation, and most completely annihilates our foreign commerce. And manufactures cannot prosper without the aid of commerce.

Some people, however, after all that has been said of the relative cheapness of our work, may still be in doubt as far as our competitive capacity in regard to England is concerned ;—the country which in Europe pays the highest wages and makes the cheapest goods. To dispel such doubts I will compare the rates paid here with those paid in Europe in the principal industries :

1. Cotton Goods—Mr. Carroll D. Wright states the average weekly wages in Lancashire and Massachusetts :

	Lancashire.	Massachusetts.	Difference.
Of weavers	$5 28	$5 64	$0 36
Of mule spinners	7 80	10 09	2 29
	$13 08	$15 73	$2 65

Considering this to be a fair average of differences paid to the various employees of the cotton mills in the respective countries, then we pay our operatives just 20 per cent. more than the English pay. And the English pay about 50 per cent. more than the Germans pay their operatives, and yet we are exporters of cotton goods to both Germany [1] and England. The figures of Mr. Wright find contradiction from various quarters. Mr. J. Chase, member of Congress from Rhode Island, himself a cotton manufacturer, places the difference as high as 62 per cent.

According to the last Census, however, the average wages for all cotton mill-hands are $246 for the year, or $4.73 a week,[2] which would imply earnings below those given by Mr. Wright. It is doubtful whether our cotton-goods operatives earn more than the English. Granting, however, for argument's sake, that they earn 25 per cent. more, then this surplus of earnings is more than balanced by longer working hours—60 hours constituting a week in Massachusetts (other States, having no legal limitation, work

[1] This we are able to do, notwithstanding Germany's tariff of 40 marks or $10 on the hundred-weight of cotton goods. 100 lbs. German weight equals 110 lbs. American.

[2] Where the annual average of earnings in any specified industry is given, it must be borne in mind, that this includes high and low wages, salaries of clerks, etc., which reduces the individual earnings of the largest proportion of workers to a sum materially below the average.

longer hours yet), against 54 to 56 hours in England, and by higher speed and greater perfection of our productive methods. But let us waive all the advantages derived from these points and take 20 per cent. as representing the proportion of wages to the product of the cotton mills, then a tariff of 5 per cent. on cotton piece-goods would cover the whole difference in the earnings of our operatives. The old tariff taxed cotton goods 35 per cent. where *ad-valorem* rates were imposed. The new tariff raised this to 40 per cent.[1] Specific rates were reduced somewhat, but not sufficiently to compensate for the great decline in the price of cotton that has taken place since 1865. Unbleached, from 5 cents to 4 cents per square yard! Bleached, from 5½ to 5 cents! on goods counting over 200 threads to the square inch. These comprise all fine goods such as nainsooks, mulls, lawns, etc., which are largely used by American manufacturers of lace goods and trimmings, who in most instances have to pay more for duties on their materials than on the finished goods of their respective branches.

2. Iron and Steel—(*a*) Pig-iron: Mr. Joseph D. Weeks, of Pittsburgh, one of our best experts, gives the price paid for labor in Pittsburgh to make a ton of pig-iron:

Labor on mining ore for ton of pig-iron @ $1.40 =		$2 38
" " " coal and making coke necessary for ton of pig-iron . . .		1 25
" " " limestone		30
" at furnace		1 25
		$5 18

In Cleveland, England, $3.17 is paid, against $5.18 in Pittsburgh. This leaves $2.01 more pay for all the workingmen that are employed in raising the ore, the coal, and the limestone and making the iron. To offset this, in addition to the transportation expenses, commission charges, etc., of from $5 to $6 on a ton of pig-iron, the tariff gives $6.72, which is a total of $12 to $13 protection. The ruling price in England of pig-iron was last year, 1882,

---

[1] This includes cotton velvets, embroideries, laces, etc., which are all raised from 35 to 40 per cent.

48s. to 50s., or say, in round figures, $12 ; the price of American pig No. 1 about $25. Now the price for Cleveland (English) pig is 40s. to 43s. For American pig in Pittsburgh $18 to $20 for No. 2, and $21 to $22 for No. 1. (*b*) Steel rails and other steel, bars, rods, etc.: Product, 983,039 tons, at an outlay for wages of $4,930,009, or $5.01½ for each ton produced. This is what the American workingman gets. Protection on rails, now $17, against the former, $28. According to Leone Levi, the English statistician, and Mr. Edward Young, the former Chief of our Bureau of Statistics, the average wages in English steel works were about 32s. or about $8 a week for skilled labor, or $1.35 a day, and 21s. a week for unskilled labor, or 87 cents a day. This gives the American steel-worker 73 per cent. more than his English brother gets. This, however, is offset, as shown before, by our better and quicker methods of manufacture. But granting, for argument's sake, even 50 per cent. more as cost of labor in this country, then this would add to the cost of a ton of American steel the magnificent sum of $1.67 for wages as against $28 or $17, respectively of protection for the mill-owners. Protection that is granted by freight and other charges on the imported stuff ought not to be lost sight of in this instance either.

"3. Leather—upper leather and calfskin manufacture—Tanner's wages—Eastern and Western cities of the United States, $10 to $11 per week. Curriers' wages—Eastern and Western cities of the United States, $14 to $15 per week. In country towns of the United States, $2 to $3 a week less. Morocco leather—Tanners' wages—New York, $12 a week ; Philadelphia, $12 a week ; Wilmington, Del., $10 a week ; Lynn, Mass., $10 a week.

" Morocco finishing by machinery—Wages of finishers—New York, $13 to $14 per week ; Philadelphia, $13 to $14 per week ; Lynn, Mass., $11 to $12 per week.

" Sole-leather tanners—In the country towns of the United States, $1.25 per day ; in Philadelphia, Baltimore, Louisville, Cincinnati, and Chicago, $9 to $10.50 per week, ten hours a day ; in London, England, $8.50 to $9.50 per week, nine hours a day's work ; in the country towns of England and in Scotland, $6 a week, nine hours a day's work ; in Germany, 80 cents to $1 a day, ten hours a day's work ; in French provinces, $5 to $5.50 a week ; in Paris (France), $1 a day.

" Sole-leather curriers—In country towns of the United States, $1.50 to $1.60 a day, ten hours a day ; in London, England, $10 to $13 a week, nine hours a day ; in the country towns of England and in Scotland, $7 to $7.50 a week ; in Leeds, England, East India tanned skins, $6.50 to $7.50 a week ; in Germany, $1 to $1.15 a day, ten hours a day ; in the provinces of France, $5 to $6 a week ; in Paris, $9 a week."

The above is an abstract of a report made by the *Shoe and Leather Reporter* to Mr. Nimmo. The correctness of the list is confirmed by twelve business firms in the line. It will be seen that the wages, considerably higher than in Germany and France, are not much above the average wages paid in England : for tanning say 12½ per cent.; while curriers get about 30 per cent. more. As the American, however, has ten working hours against the Englishman's nine hours, the surplus added to the cost of production on account of higher wages is reduced in tanning to a minimum—less than 5 per cent.; in currying to about 15 per cent.

As wages determine only a correspondingly small part of the value of the whole product, it is evident that this industry can afford to do without the paternal care of the Government. We are heavy exporters of leather. Hides are not protected. The lord of the prairie, the aristocratic ox, under a democratic form of government does not enjoy the protection that is extended to his plebeian cousin, the sheep.

4. Silk goods—The difference in wages varies largely between the different European countries—England, Germany, France, and Switzerland. A statement of wages and earnings would give a very inadequate idea. The various modes of operation have to be taken into consideration. The greater efficiency of the workers, and the application of most improved machinery, to a large extent obliterate the influence of higher earnings on cost of product. Americans earn from 65 to 75 per cent. more than the English ; perhaps 100 per cent. more than German operatives. The acknowledged superiority of our working methods reduces the difference materially : 50 per cent., as an addition of cost, would be a very high estimate. Many of our silks are produced in New

Jersey, whose product in 1880 was $13,850,000 (cost) ; of this there was paid in wages $4,177,000, or 30 per cent.; 50 per cent. of 30 per cent. is equal to 15 per cent. All the protection needed to protect the workingman is 15 per cent. A tariff of 50 per cent. is certainly excessive, in view of the enjoyment of free raw silk. A tariff of 30 per cent., with free materials, would give ample protection to the silk manufacturer. It is doubtful whether the present rate of protection amounts to much more than that, considering the latitude under-valuation and smuggling enjoyed under the former tariff. The reduction to 50 per cent. still gives ample opportunities for these practices.

5. Woollens—From the report of the United States Consul at Leeds the following may be taken as ruling prices in 1878, the week having 54 working-hours against not less than 60 hours in America :

Wool-sorters per week	$6 24 to $6 72
Scourers and dyers per week	4 80 to 5 75
Spinners per week	7 70 to 9 69
Weavers, men, per week	6 00 to 8 40
Weavers, women, per week	3 60 to 4 80
Pressers per week	5 75 to 6 72
Laborers per week	4 32 to 5 25

Considering the difference in time, I doubt whether our woollen mills pay much more in wages for a given piece of work than the English. $4.50 to $6.00 for women and $6.00 to $9.00 for men are fair average wages of operatives in American woollen mills. Still we have a specific and an *ad-valorem* duty to pay on woollens, averaging fully 60 per cent. even after the reduction.

Now, I ask any candid manufacturer whether his " infant " industry would not be fully protected with a tariff of 25 per cent., plain and simple, if he had wool and other raw materials free of duty? With free raw materials he could build up an export trade and thereby give more steady employment to his help.

6. Coal, anthracite—In 1880 we mined 27,433,000 tons, and paid in wages $21,680,000, or 79 cents a ton.

Coal, bituminous—Product, 40,311,000 tons ; wages, $30,707,-000, or 76 cents on the average a ton, Pennsylvania producing 18,000,000 tons, at a cost of only 64 cents a ton for wages.

I leave the intelligent reader to determine for himself whether a protective tariff of 75 cents is required to secure to the working-man 64 cents in wages.

The average wages of miners in Scotland are four shillings a day.

These examples must suffice. If I have not succeeded, from statistics introduced, in proving the absurdity of the claim of protectionists—

(1) That we cannot compete with Europe, provided we have free raw materials ;

(2) That the tariff protects our working people ; and

(3) That the tariff protects our industries ; then no amount of argument will prove it.

The remedy for all evils lies in the hands of the voters. Like voters, like law-makers. It will not do to shift the blame on other shoulders. This is a free government, and the cure for all abuses must come from the people. No question is so important with respect to the welfare of a people as the question of taxation. The equitable adjustment of taxes is the foundation of universal prosperity. Unequal taxation enriches the few and impoverishes the millions. Nothing stands in the way to prevent Congress from entering into an immediate settlement of this most important question.

Why, then, dig in the sepulchres of the past for dry bones and dead issues ?

The old political feuds are settled. We stand before a new era. The solution of economic questions is demanded by the rising generation, a generation which has lost the meaning even of the old catchwords.

Besides, we have turned a page in our history. We have become a great manufacturing nation. The narrow confines in which the tariff encircles us must give way before the all-over-powering energy of a young nation. A thorough revision of the tariff upon the basis of free raw materials has become an urgent necessity for the preservation of our vast manufacturing industries.

EXPLANATORY REMARKS TO TABLES.

APPENDIX I shows the tariffs of Great Britain, Canada, Germany, France, Belgium, Netherlands, and the United States, so far as they refer to manufacturing industries, and to raw materials used in the respective industries. I also give a statement of imports and exports coming under these headings, both in the aggregate and per capita of population of each country. It will be seen that, excepting the United States, all import their raw materials free of duty, whether they possess rich mines, as England, Germany, and Belgium, or whether they are large sheep-raisers themselves, such as England and Germany. The result of this policy is, that they all do a large exporting trade in manufacturing products, regardless of respective policies of free trade or protection in manufacturing industries; England under free trade doing the largest share of exports, and per capita almost the smallest of imports, in merchandise, which she admits free of duty, while all other nations impose duties more or less heavy on them. The United States, with highest import duties, are the heaviest importers of manufactured goods, so heavily taxed that the duties are more than double those of any of the other protecting nations. Her exports are almost *nil*, for the simple reason that America is the only country which taxes raw materials, as will be seen from the tables.

The Netherlands are heavy importers of manufactured goods; among her imports of textiles, yarns form a very heavy item. They have no mines, and metals are therefore a very important class of imports. The Netherlands have a largely developed commerce, while manufacturing industries are behind those of adjacent countries. This in spite of the lowness of wages and the lower standard of life of their working-classes, to which fact I call special attention in support of the position taken in Chapter X.

The foreign commerce in the principal manufactures, textiles and metal goods, of the different nations, shows :

| COUNTRIES. | Imports. | | Exports. | |
	Total.	Per Head.	Total.	Per Head.
1. England . . .	$148,000,000.	$4 22	$804,000,000.	$22 94
2. Germany . .	57,000,000.	1 27	284,000,000.	6 31
3. France . . .	83,500,000.	2 24	182,600,000.	4 91
4. Netherlands . .	69,750,000.	17 44	49,200,000.	12 30
5. United States . .	212,500,000.	4 11	44,800,000.	86

It will be seen that the imports of the United States in manufactures which they endeavor so strongly to exclude by abnormally high duties, exceed those of Germany, France, and the Netherlands combined, or those of England and Germany, while their exports do not even reach those of the Netherlands with barely one tenth of the population of the United States. If we except cotton goods, machinery, arms, tools, and the like, the total is less than ten millions, or seven cents per capita.

The percentage of labor and material in these metal goods is as follows :

ARTICLES.	Labor.	Material.
Agricultural implements	33 %	67 %
Cutlery	49 %	51 %
Fire-arms	60 %	40 %
Sewing-machines	49½ %	50½ %
Foundry produce, machinery . . .	40 %	60 %

The relation of labor to material in the iron and steel industries, pig-iron, bar iron, rails, etc., is 22 % labor, and 78 % material; a convincing proof that it is the cost of the material and not the labor cost that stands in our way and causes a state of affairs which must bring a blush to our face, when we compare the eighty-six cents of our exports with $22.94 of England, and the three millions of American tonnage with the twenty millions of English tonnage, illustrative of the decay of our foreign commerce.[1]

[1] See Note on page 88.

In specific tariff rates the averages are given wherever the rates differ largely on various subdivisions of the same class of goods.

The exports of free trade of England in manufactures are more than five times as large as her imports in the same classes, and exceed by far the combined exports of all other commercial nations, including the United States. In general merchandise, however, her imports are largely in excess of her exports. This large excess of English imports over exports is frequently commented upon by protectionists as a sign of future calamity. In 1880, it amounted to about $600,000,000. This excess shows, on the contrary, the wealth and great financial strength of England, and is practically a national profit made up as follows :

Freightage to and from foreign countries in the sum of	$215,000,000
Interest on foreign investments	265,000,000
Ships sold	7,000,000
Commissions on foreign trade	80,000,000
Interest on foreign trade	23,000,000
Total	$590,000,000

APPENDIX II shows the revenue systems of the commercial nations named. The United States derive their income solely from excise- and customs-duties, which bear heaviest on the working-classes as consumers of their entire income. All other nations obtain large sums from income- and stamp-taxes, that come mostly from accumulated property.

In APPENDIX III I place the old and the new (1883) tariffs of the United States side by side. The two tariffs are necessarily represented only in the most important classes. As I found it impossible to go into the details and subdivisions of each branch, the work is necessarily incomplete. It is, however, sufficient to show the entire inadequacy of the so-called "tariff reform" as a measure of relief to our industries. Some items of duties are largely raised, as, for instance, all-wool dress goods, for which a new classification has been created, to "encourage" the making of cashmeres. But the increase of duty, this patent medicine for all ills of American growth, does not cover the defects of American wools, which so far have not produced the soft textures of the French article.

APPENDIX IV shows the *ad-valorem* equivalent of specific duties at different periods under changing prices. While foreign prices in iron, steel, and in raw wool have declined, the specific rates have remained, consequently the percentage of duties, even after the revision of 1883, is heavier than it was twelve years ago.

NOTE.—In 1860 our foreign commerce amounted to $762,000,000, of which were carried in *American bottoms* $507,000,000, or 66%, and *foreign bottoms* 255,000,000, or 34%.

In 1880 our commerce had risen to $1,589.000,000, of which were carried in *American bottoms* $280,000,000, or 17%, and *foreign bottoms* 1,309,000,000, or 83%. In 1870 we carried yet $352.000,000 in American ships. The great expansion of our foreign commerce benefited foreign shipping only. Within twenty years our foreign trade rose from eight and a quarter to eighteen million tons, or 120%; and while our share of these eight and a quarter million tons was six millions, or 70% of tonnage in 1860, the same had declined in 1880 to so low a level that of eighteen millions our share was only three and two-fifth millions, or 19%.

			1.
			2.
			3.
			4.
			5.
	$4,800,000	}	6.
			7.
	1,000,000		8.
	3,600,000		9.
.18	$190,000	.004	10.
.63	900,000	.02	11.
.39	200,000	.004	12.
.04	2,100,000	.04	13.
.06	23,000,000	.44	14.
.008	700,000	.014	15.
.67	13,000,000	.25	16.
.73	408,000	.008	17.
.75			18.
.45	700,000	.014	19.
.10	2,400,000	.046	20.
.10	1,200,000	.023	21.
4.11	$44,800,000	.86	

APPENDIX II.—Showing how the nations named in Appendix I raise their revenues. 1882. .000 omitted.

Classes of Net Income.	Great Britain.	Germany.	France.	Netherlands.	United States.
1. Customs	$95,000	$46,000	$63,000	$2,000	$195,000
2. Excise	135,000	38,000	190,000	14,000	130,000
3. Stamp tax . . .	60,000	4,900	140,000	9,000	
4. Land tax	5,000		²10,000		
5. House duty . . .	8,500				
6. Income tax, etc. . .	50,000	¹	³90,000	10,000	
7. Post-office . . .	13,600	} 5,100	22,000	1,750	⁴2,100
8. Telegraph . . .	4,900	}	5,000	400	
9. Crown lands, interest, etc.	8,500			700	1,000
10. Miscellaneous . . .	20,000	10,500	20,000	3,000	13,000
11. Railroads . . .		3,100		800	⁵4,000
12. Contribution of States .		25,000			
13. Extraordinary . . .		12,000			
14. National banks . .					7,100
	$396,500	$144,600	$540,100	$41,650	$352,200

¹ State tax.   ² Forests.   ³ All direct taxes included.
⁴ Excess of income   ⁵ Pacific R. R. reimbursements.

ARTICLES.	Tariff of 1870.			Tariff of 1883.		
	Specific.	Ad Valorem.	Equal to Per Cent.	Specific.	Ad Valorem.	Equal to Per Cent.
SCHEDULE A—Chemicals.		%			%	
Glue, beeswax			20			20
Soap, sponges			20			20
Sumac, ammonia			20			20
Cement, cobalt			20			
Turpentine, spirits of . gal.	.30					20
Extracts of indigo			20			10
Soap . . . . lb.	1c.	+30				20
Mineral waters			30			30
Coal-tar colors . lb.	.50	+35				35
Logwood and other dyewood extracts			10			10
Colors and paints .			25			25
Preparations of essential oils, etc.	Mostly specific.					25
All crude barks, etc., or minerals .			20			Free.
Advanced or prepared			40			10
Other chemicals paid specific rates, varying and too extended for classification here . . . . lb.				1 to 10c.		
SCHEDULE B.						
Brown earthenware			25			25
China, porcelain, etc. .			45			60
All other earthenware .			40			55
Stoneware above ten-gallon capacity			20			20
Tiles .			35			35
Bricks .			20			20
Bottles .			35			40
Cut-glass bottles .			40			45
Other glass .	3 to 50			3 to 50c.		
" silvered	4 to 60			4 to 60c.		
SCHEDULE C—Metals.						
Iron ore . . . ton			20	75c.		27½
Pig-iron . . . "	$7 00		66⅔	$6 72		64

ARTICLES.	Tariff of 1870.			Tariff of 1883.		
	Specific.	Ad Valorem.	Equal to Per Cent.	Specific.	Ad Valorem.	Equal to Per Cent.
		%			%	
Bar and other iron . ton	22 40 to 33.60		80	17.60 to 33.60		75
Steel rails	28.00		108	17.00		65
" blooms . . .			30			45
" n. o. p. . . .			30			45
Iron manufactures . .			35			45
Steel " . . .			45			45
Copper ore . . lb.	3c.			2½c.		
" pigs or bars . .	5c.			4c.		
" manufactures . .			45			45
Gold " . .			35 to 40			45
Silver " . .			40			45
Cutlery . . .			35			45

SCHEDULE I—Cotton Goods.

Woven fabrics, not exceeding 200 threads to square inch :						
Unbleached square yard	5c.			3c.		
Bleached . . " "	5⅛c.	+20		4c.		
Dyed . . " "	5½c.			5c.		
Valued over 16 cents .			35			
" " 8c. unbleached						40
" " 10c. bleached .						
" " 13c. dyed .						
Exceeding 200 threads to square inch :						
Unbleached square yard	5c.			4c.		
Bleached . . " "	5⅛c.	+20		5c.		
Dyed . . " "	5½c.			6c.		
Shirts, drawers, stocking narrowed on frames . .			35			40
Cotton velvets . . .			35			40
Laces and embroideries .			35			40
Spool cotton, dozen 100-yard spools	6c.	+30		7c.		

SCHEDULE J—Hemp, Jute, and Flax.

Flax straw . . . ton	$5 00			$5 00		
" not hackled . . .	20 00			20 00		
" hackled, etc. . .	40 00			40 00		

ARTICLES.	Tariff of 1870.			Tariff of 1883.		
	Specific	Ad Valorem.	Equal to Per Cent.	Specific.	Ad Valorem.	Equal to Per Cent.
Hemp and jute, same in both tariffs.						
Linen, brown and bleached .			30			35
Over 30c. square yard .			35			35
Thread for carpets, etc., at						
24c. or less . . .			30			40
Over 24c.			35			40
Other			40			40
Grass cloth			30			35
Burlaps			35			30
SCHEDULE K—Wool and Woollens.						
Wool under 30c. . . .				10c.		
" over 30c. . . .				12c.		
" under 32c. . . .	10c.	+11				
" over 32c. . . .	12c.	+10				
Shoddy, rags, waste, etc. lb.	12c.			10c.		
Woollen cloth, shawls . "	50c.	+35	75 to 150	35c.	+35	80 to 115
Above 80c. . . "	50c.	+35	50 to 75	35c.	+40	50 to 80
Flannels, blankets, hats, knit goods . . .	Varying rate according to value, both specific and *ad valorem,* averaging		95	averaging		70
Cotton warp dress goods :						
Under 20c. sq. yard, sq. yd.	6c.	+35	65	5c.	+35	60
Above " " "	8c.	+40	78	7c.	+40	73
All wool dress goods :						
Under 20c. sq. yard, sq. yd.	6c.	+35	65	9c.	+40	88
Above " " " (Say 30 cents.)	8c.	+35	60	9c.	+40	70
Clothing, ready-made . lb.	50c.	+40		40c.	+35	
Cloaks, dolmans, etc. . "	50c.	+40	50 to 90	45c.	+40	49 to 85
SCHEDULE L—Silk.						
Raw silk . . .	Free.			Free.		

ARTICLES.	Tariff of 1870.			Tariff of 1883.		
	Specific.	Ad Valorem.	Equal to Per Cent.	Specific.	Ad Valorem.	Equal to Per Cent.
		%			%	
Thrown silk .			35			40
Sewing silk, etc. .			40			40
Silk goods .			60			50
SCHEDULE M—Books, Papers.						
Books, printed .			25			25
" blank .			25			20
Printing paper .			20			15
Paper manufactures, n. o. p. .			35			15
Paper boxes .			35			35
Paper hangings, etc. .			35			25
Paper pulp .			20			10
SCHEDULE N—Sundries.						
Leather, bend, sole, etc. .			35			15
Calfskin, tanned, dressed, etc.			30			25
Leather, manufactures .			35			35
Paintings .			10			30
Statuary .			10			30
Papier-maché .			35			30
Umbrellas .			50			40
" silk .			60			50
Coal . ton	75c.			75c.		50
Feathers .			35			50
Gloves .			50			50
Hatter's plush .			25			25

www.ingramcontent.com/pod-product-compliance
Lightning Source LLC
Chambersburg PA
CBHW032153010726
47493CB00008BA/2685